TO LIVE IS CHRIST

Paul's Message of Salvation

T. A. Kantonen

TO LIVE IS CHRIST

Copyright © MCMLXXVII by
The C.S.S. Publishing Company, Inc.
Lima, Ohio

ISBN 0-89536-306-2   PRINTED IN U.S.A.

To my colleagues
Amos John Traver and Willard Dow Allbeck,
teachers and exemplars of life in Christ

TABLE OF CONTENTS

FOREWORD

In the fall of 1976 I was invited to deliver a series of lectures to the Northwest Ohio School of Continuing Education for Pastors and Priests, held at Winebrenner Theological Seminary in Findlay, Ohio. The theme assigned to me was "Grace, Redemption, and Salvation in the Pauline Epistles." In response to requests by those who heard the lectures they are now published in revised and abridged form.

Amid the various efforts to adapt the Christian message to the changing conditions of our time, there is evidence of a growing desire to obtain anew a clear and firm grasp of the basic content of the message itself. No one is a more dependable guide in this effort than Paul, the first Christian theologian, the man who gave the original message its conceptual form.

The task of presenting the basics of Pauline theology was, of course, congenial to a Lutheran theologian, but interest in this subject has no denominational limitations. In fact, the theme of the lectures was proposed by a Roman Catholic member of the ecumenical committee which arranged the presentation.

The study relies as its primary source upon Paul's own letters, quoted chiefly in the Revised Standard Version. The secondary sources to which I am most deeply indebted are Archibald M. Hunter's **The Gospel According to St. Paul**, Rudolf Bultmann's **Theology of the New Testament**, E. Earle Ellis' **Paul and His Recent Interpreters**, C. H. Dodd's **The Meaning of Paul for Today**, and Oscar Cullmann's **The Christology of the New Testament**.

This book is by its origin primarily a book for pastors, but I am convinced that it can be understood also by thinking laypersons. They should

8

not be intimidated by the use of Paul's Greek words such as "agape" and "parousia" or of theological terms such as "eschatology," for their meaning in English is explained.

Paul continues to direct the preaching and teaching of the church to its living center, the crucified and risen Christ. If this little book can point the way in this direction, it will serve its purpose.

With further explanation and discussion the book may be put to use as a study book for adult groups. For this purpose it is accompanied by a **Teacher's Guide.**

t. a. k.

CHAPTER ONE

Paul: The Man and His Message

Hans Lietzmann, noted New Testament scholar, once remarked that no one has correctly understood Jesus except Paul and no one has correctly understood Paul. The attempts to understand Paul are legion. The literature on him is immense and the interpretations of his thought are varied. To Bultmann he is "the founder of Christian theology," while to Morton Enslin he is not a theologian at all but simply a "practical and forthright man" who taught new life in Christ but had little regard for logical consistency. In any case, his whole world of thought, whether or not its complexities can be fitted into a coherent system, revolves around the axis "for me to live is Christ" (Philippians 1:21). The dominant motif of his message is the saving activity of God in the person and work of Christ, particularly in his death and resurrection. The purpose of the present study is to examine the fundamental emphases growing out of this motif and to apply them to our day.

First-hand source material for understanding Paul's message is provided by the letters (epistles) which he wrote to his converts. Especially important are the primary doctrinal epistles, Romans, Galatians, and First and Second Corinthians, and it is upon them that our study is chiefly based. Theologically significant also is Ephesians, which is an authentic summary of Paul's thought, even though many scholars question whether the apostle himself wrote it. Some valuable insights are derived also from First Thessalonians and Philippians, which are undoubtedly genuine letters of Paul. The letter to Philemon is likewise genuine, but it contributes little to his basic theology. Such is not the case with Colossians and Second Thessalonians, the authorship of which remains controversial but which are Pauline in content. The consensus of biblical scholarship today accepts as valid sources of Pauline thought all the letters traditionally ascribed to him, with the exception of the Pastorals, namely, First and Second Timothy and Titus. The case for the later origin of the Pastorals is too strong to be refuted.

Paul the Man

We cannot understand Paul's theology without understanding the personality and the personal religious experience of the man himself. Until the 19th century, Paul was generally regarded as an authentic representative of original Christianity, whose dramatic conversion experience transformed the foremost enemy of Christ into his foremost protagonist and whose intellectual talents enabled him to become the man who gave the Christian gospel its conceptual form. But with the rise of biblical criticism and the history of religion this view was challenged. Baur and the old Tuebingen school sought to point out the difference between Jesus and Paul and to present Paul as the founder of a new kind of Christianity. Harnack contended that while the center of the teaching of Jesus was the Father, the center of Paul's thinking was Christ. The "history of religion" school, Troeltsch and others, insisted that Paul was an extraordinary religious genius who poured forth his own casual feelings but constructed no consistent theology. Contemporary research tends to affirm the earlier view and to reject the extremes of nineteenth century speculation. The chief problems still under debate are: Was Paul primarily a Jew or a Hellenist? Is the key to his theology to be found in eschatology or in mysticism?

Little is known concerning Paul's life from his birth to his appearance in Jerusalem as a persecutor of Christians. We know from references in the epistles and in **Acts** that he was of the tribe of Benjamin and a zealous member of the Pharisee party. He was born in Tarsus in Cilicia, which was truly "no mean city," as Paul himself says. It was a center of Hellenic culture and learning, and during his youth Paul evidently became acquainted with various Greek philosophies and religious cults. He and his family were Roman citizens, which, together with his education and early rise to prominence, suggests some measure of means and status. But the Jewish background was also strong. Paul tells us that he was "brought up in Jerusalem at the feet of Gamaliel, educated according to the strict manner of the law of our fathers" (Acts 22:3). He was a fervent champion of the traditions of the fathers, and while still a young man was given authority to direct the persecution of Christians. He was apparently a member of the Sanhedrin, for he speaks of casting his vote in the trial of Christians (Acts 26:10).

Concerning Paul's personal appearance, canonical Scriptures suggest only that it was not impressive, but the account in the apocryphal **Acts of Paul and Thecla**, credited by such scholars as Deissmann and Ramsay, is more vivid: "And he saw Paul coming, a man of little stature, thin haired upon the head, crooked in the legs, of good state of body, with eyebrows joining, and nose somewhat hooked, full of grace: for sometimes he appeared like a man, and sometimes he had the face of an angel."

The outstanding trait of Paul's personality is an indomitable will. Whether as persecutor of Christians or as campaigner for Christ, he is a zealot. His missionary career is marked by "great endurance, in afflictions, hardships, calamities, beatings, imprisonments, tumults, labors, watching, hunger" (2 Corinthians 6:4-5). When he lists in detail the obstacles he had to conquer (2 Corinthians 11), he is inclined "to boast a little," confident that humanly speaking his boasting is based on solid achievements and that he is "not in the least inferior" to anyone else. Whatever "thorn in the flesh" afflicts him, he uses it as a handle for getting a firmer grip on the grace of God. He is so sure of his stand that he dares to rebuke Peter, the acknowledged leader of the Christian community (Galatians 2:11-14). That he could not always control his temper is indicated by his abrupt dismissal of his colleague, Mark (Acts 15:38).

But natural inclinations did not hold the reins in the conduct of the "new man in Christ." A proud and solitary man becomes a gentle father to his spiritual "children," so beloved that some were willing to risk their lives for him (Romans 16:4, Philippians 2:30). Himself a celibate, he has a highly sublimated view of marriage, comparing a wife's relation to her husband to the church's relation to Christ. Nor does his own asceticism prevent him from acknowledging the sexual basis of marriage. Continence is not the norm. Sexual relations are to be interrupted only for periods of prayer and then resumed (1 Corinthians 7:5). Not only does he understand human nature but he also feels a deep empathy for the whole human race, "groaning inwardly" (Romans 8:23) and "sighing with anxiety" (2 Corinthians 5:4) over its distress. Yet the dominant note in his own experience and in his message to others is "Rejoice in the Lord always" (Philippians 4:4).

In the structure of his personality Paul resembles the great prophets of the Old Testament. He too has ecstatic visions and an overpowering consciousness of having been called to communicate divine revelation. Like Jeremiah, he knows that he has been set apart even before he was born (Galatians 1:15) and that an inner compulsion to deliver God's message has been laid upon him (1 Corinthians 9:16).

Paul was a Jew but he was a Hellenistic Jew. The hooked nose is a symbol of his Jewishness, the angelic face of Hellenistic ecstasy. The source of Paul's theology cannot be expressed by a single word: **either** Jewish eschatology **or** Hellenic mysticism. It is **both**. And the two become united in a profound personal religious experience which transforms a Jewish zealot into a Christian apostle. Paul's conversion experience represents on the one hand the failure of salvation through the law and the discovery of a new way, salvation by grace, and on the other hand mystical union with the living Christ. Thus the background of Paul's theology is threefold: Greek, Jewish, and Christian.

The Background

Turning first to the Greek background, Paul's debt to Hellenism cannot be denied. The Bible which he used was the Septuagint, the Greek translation of the Old Testament, the Bible of the apostolic church. He wrote his letters in the **koine,** the common Greek which was the international language of the day. Most of his ministry was in places dominated by Greek culture and civilization. He quotes Greek poets, Aratus, "We are also his offspring" (Acts 17:28) and Menander, "Bad company ruins good morals" (1 Corinthians 15:33). He draws illustrations from Greek games, running, boxing, wrestling, the arena, and from the Graeco-Roman processes of law, such as "adoption." Unlike other New Testament writers, he uses words from Greek moral philosophy, such as

14

"virtue" and "conscience" and "law written on the heart," the Stoic doctrine of innate knowledge of the principles of right and wrong. He resorts to the language of the devotees of the Greek mystery cults, speaking of initiation and mystery, and, like them, is given to visions and ecstasies.

Gilbert Murray, eminent literary scholar, is thus led to describe Paul as "one of the great figures of Greek literature." But many theologians have also emphasized the Hellenic-mystical aspect of Paul's thought. In opposition to the Augustinian-Lutheran-Barthian line of thought which makes justification by grace Paul's central theme, Wrede contended in the beginning of the present century that justification was only an incidental polemical issue developed in the controversy with the Judaizers, while Christ-centered mysticism, "being in Christ," was central. Deissmann, Bousset, Heitmueller, and others have followed this line. Schweitzer, too, stresses Paul's mysticism but regards it as unique rather than typically Hellenic. Dying with Christ and being raised with him into a new life is basic, but it is better described as Jewish eschatological mysticism. According to Bultmann, on the other hand, Paul must be viewed within the framework of Hellenistic Christianity. He was won to the Christian faith by the proclamation of the Hellenistic church and he was an advocate of Hellenistic Christianity over against the Palestinian church.

While Paul's Hellenistic background must be acknowledged, neither must it be over-emphasized. He was, after all, according to his own description, "a Hebrew of the Hebrews" (Philippians 3:5), a Hebrew born and bred. In the words of Archibald Hunter, "Though the surface of Paul's thought may owe much to Hellenism, its sub-soil remained Jewish."[1] With the devout Jews of his time he believed in the one holy and righteous God, in the election of Israel to be his special people, in the Law as the unique revelation of God and his will for man, and in the hope of the Messiah. His basic thinking remains Jewish throughout. He sees history not as the eternal recurrence of the Greek view, but in the perspective of the prophets as the scene of purposeful divine operation from creation to final consummation. Jewish is his antithesis between flesh and spirit as well as the idea of corporate personality, which leads him to speak of being in the first Adam and in the last Adam. The Christian hope for him is not the Greek immortality of the soul but the Hebrew resurrection of the body. And when he speaks of the consummation of God's purpose in history, he concludes with "And so all Israel will be saved" (Romans 11:26).

Turning now to the specific Christian background, we must note that while Paul had no contact with the historical Jesus himself, he did have Christian kinsmen. "Greet Andronicus and Junias," he says, "my kinsmen and my fellow-prisoners; they are men of note among the apostles, and they were in Christ before me" (Romans 16:7). And his experience of the martyrdom of Stephen must have made a deep impression upon him. He was the young man at whose feet the participants in the stoning laid their garments and who "consented to the death." But he could not erase from his memory the image of the martyr who in dying gazed into heaven and saw the glory of God and the Son of Man standing at the right hand of God, and prayed, "Lord, do not hold this sin against them" (Acts 7:58-60). Some psychologists in fact have interpreted the Damascus road experience as the re-appearance of this image from Paul's subconscious mind.

But the roots of Paul's gospel of salvation by grace go deeper than any single incident. They are to be traced, first of all, to the Hebrew Scriptures. While the dominant interpretation of these Scriptures in Paul's day was legalistic, there are scholars, both Jewish and Christian, who find the central motif of the Old Testament to be **chesed ve emet**, the grace of the covenant. The existence and destiny of Israel depended on the sheer grace of God, not on the nation's own merit. "Know, therefore, that the Lord your God is not giving you this good land to possess because of your righteousness, for you are a stubborn people." "It is because he loves you" (Deuteronomy 9:6; 7:8). This is what the prophets proclaim. The guilt of sin must be removed, declares Isaiah, before a true relation to God is possible. The message of Hosea is that sin brings about unworthiness and breaks the covenant relationship, but God loves sinful Israel. During the Exile the concept of grace is deepened. Thus, according to Deutero-Isaiah, God's righteousness is consummated in forgiveness, in the redeeming love that saves from judgment. "In overflowing wrath for a moment I hid my face from you, but with everlasting love I will have compassion on you, says the Lord, your Redeemer" (Isaiah 54:8).

The grace note sounds clearly in the **kerygma** (the proclaimed message) of the Hellenic church, upon which Paul's theology is chiefly grounded. The Jesus of the Christian proclamation declares, "I came not to call the righteous but sinners" (Matthew 9:13). Paul's own disciple, Luke, transmits the astounding story about a lost son, comparing God to a father who lavishes his affection upon a moral derelict whose only claim to consideration is his utter helplessness (Luke 15). In another illustration, Jesus draws a sharp contrast between a Pharisee, a devout keeper of the law, and a tax-gatherer, self-condemned before the law and appealing only to God's mercy. Jesus concludes, "This man (the latter) went down to his house justified rather than the other" (Luke 18:14). Here the term "justified" (dedikaiomenos) is used in the precise Pauline sense of being acceptable to God, and the way of justification is shown to be the way of grace as distinguished from the way of the law.

The divine love which freely pours itself upon the undeserving shines in its full glory from the cross, where the innocent Sufferer prays for his crucifiers and with his pierced hand opens the door to paradise to a dying criminal. After the disciples had experienced the reality of the resurrection of their Lord, reflection upon the whole drama of the cross could not fail to disclose new depths of meaning in the words he had spoken earlier, "The Son of man came . . . to give his life as a ransom for many" (Matthew 20:28) and "My blood . . . poured for many for the forgiveness of sins" (Matthew 26:28). Here, then, is the richest source for Paul's doctrine of grace, redemption, and salvation, summarized in such an assertion as this: "Since all have sinned and fall short of the glory of God, they are justified by his grace as a gift, through the redemption which is in Christ Jesus, whom God put forward as an expiation by his blood, to be received by faith" (Romans 3:23-25).

It is a mistake, then, to stress, as Baur and Harnack did, the difference between Paul's theology and the message of the original apostles. Paul himself says, "I delivered to you as of first importance what I also received, (that is, from the common Christian tradition) that Christ died for our sins in accordance with the scriptures, that he was raised on the third day in accordance with the scriptures." Then he adds, significantly enough, "Whether then it was I or they (Peter, John, James, and the others), this is what we all proclaim" (1 Corinthians 15:3-11).

Hunter lists seven basic elements in what was once called "Paulinism" but which actually stem from those who were "in Christ" before him: (1) the apostolic kerygma, (2) the confession of Jesus as Messiah, (3) the doctrine of the Holy Spirit as the divine dynamic of the new life, (4) the conception of the church as the new Israel, (5) the sacraments of baptism and the Lord's Supper, (6) the "words of the Lord" which Paul quotes or echoes in his letters, and (7) the hope of the **parousia**, Christ's return in glory.[2]

The Conversion Experience

Paul's debt to pre-Pauline Christianity is thus greater than his debt to Hellenism or Judaism. All three find expression in his theology, but the key to the theological structure which he created is to be found in his conversion experience. The importance of what happened on the Damascus road is attested by the fact that **Acts** gives us no less than three accounts of it (chapters 9, 22, and 26). Paul's theology is not a mosaic in which the various elements of his background are intellectually pieced together. It grows out of a soul-shaking and deeply emotional personal experience which completely changed the man himself. It is the theology of a converted man who found a new way of salvation, who could now say, "By the grace of God I am what I am" (1 Corinthians 15:10).

It is frequently supposed that in Romans 7 Paul himself interprets the meaning of his conversion, that the account there of the conflict between flesh and spirit, between willing and doing, of the resulting moral collapse and despair, is autobiographical. Luther, however, with a sounder exegesis of the whole context, insists that the conflict represents the experience of the converted Paul, who, like all believers, is **simul iustus et peccator**, sinner and saint at the same time. Does not Paul conclude, "So then, I of myself serve the law of God with my mind, but with my flesh I serve the law of sin"?

Bultmann, agreeing with Luther, finds Paul's true interpretation of his experience in Philippians 3, where the apostle rejects all his former values as rubbish in order to be found in Christ. In Bultmann's words, "This is what his conversion meant. In it he surrendered his previous understanding of himself, that is , he surrendered what had till then been the norm and meaning of his life, he sacrificed what had hitherto been his pride and joy ... It was obedient submission to the judgment of God, made known in the cross of Christ, upon all human accomplishment and boasting."[3]

It is in the light of this radical transvaluation of values that all aspects of Paul's theology must be understood. It took time before all the implications of the Damascus road experience became clear to him. But following the line of thought developed by Jeremias and Hunter, we may summarize thus the decisive consequences of the experience. It meant, first, that Jesus is a living reality. Paul became convinced that he was in touch with a living and exalted person and that this person was the crucified Jesus of Nazareth. Second, the cross became for him the center of divine revelation, the revelation of God's redeeming love. Before his conversion, guided by Deuteronomy 21:23: "A hanged man is accursed by God," he had said, "Jesus is accursed" (1 Corinthians 12:3). After his conversion, this was still his watchword, but now he added the words "for us." His doctrine of the atonement is summed up in Galatians 3:13: "Christ redeemed us from the curse of the law, having become a curse for us." Third, Paul discovered that salvation is a divine act of pure grace which man has done nothing to deserve. Grace became the keyword of all his theology. Jeremias attributes seven other items to Paul's conversion experience: his interpretation of predestination, his sense of sin, his opposition to legalism, his Christian hope, his missionary obligation, his apostolic authority, and his doctrine of the church.[4]

The Message and the Mission

What happened in Paul's encounter with Christ on the Damascus road is a secret between the apostle and his Lord. But its transforming and vitalizing impact upon the man and his use of his religious heritage radiates throughout his message. It was the pivotal influence in shaping the good news of salvation by grace which he proclaimed.

The message itself, however, is objective in nature and does not consist in a narration of what happened to Paul himself. Paul would not have agreed with Schleiermacher that the primary content of the kerygma is the communication by one man of his personal experience in the hope of stimulating other men to have a similar experience. Nor would he have approved the popular evangelism of our day, in which "I" looms so large. "What we preach," says Paul, "is not ourselves but Jesus Christ as Lord" (2 Corinthians 4:5).

Jesus Christ as Lord is indeed an epitome of what Paul preached. He had no personal contact with the historical Jesus but on the basis of the proclamation of the pre-Pauline church he was well acquainted with the life and teaching of Jesus. We have noted the fallacy of the view that there is a great gulf fixed between the Jesus of the Gospels and the Christ of the Pauline epistles. The Epistles, to be sure, are not Gospels and do not set out to recount "all that Jesus began to do and to teach." But when the basic content of the Christian message is seen to be not a simple moralism of the fatherhood of God and the brotherhood of man but the eschatological coming of God's kingdom, then Paul must be acknowledged to be the supreme interpreter of the gospel, the apostle who faithfully fulfills the intention of Jesus. The difference lies in the difference between the situations before and after Easter and Pentecost. Jesus had no risen and glorified Savior to proclaim, Paul did. Paul's theology, as Kümmel puts it, is faith's answer to the saving work of God which Jesus proclaimed and which to Paul was an accomplished fact.[5] Through the resurrection and exaltation of Jesus and the coming of the Holy Spirit, the kingdom of God had come and Christians already lived in the new aeon.

Paul's mission, then, was not to interpret the teachings of the Prophet of Galilee nor to describe the events which preceded his death. His concern was with the events which followed his death. To us the "life of Christ" usually means the earthly career of Jesus. To Paul it meant the life of the risen Son of God, of whom he could say, "For me to live is Christ." As for Peter on Pentecost, "this Jesus whom you crucified" was now "both Lord and Christ."

When Peter declared that God had made Jesus of Nazareth the Christ, he was applying to Jesus the title of Messiah. In preaching the gospel to the Jews Paul did the same. In Acts 9:22 we read that Paul "silenced the Jews of Damascus with his cogent proofs that Jesus was the Messiah." And in Romans 9:5 he writes, "from them (the Jews) in natural descent sprang the Messiah." Nils Dahl has shown that Paul's whole work as an apostle was conditioned by the Messiahship of Jesus. But since Paul was primarily the apostle to the Gentiles, to whom the Messianic hope of the Jews was less meaningful, he made little effort to prove to them that Jesus was the promised Messiah; Christ, the Greek equivalent of Messiah, became in his letters a proper name rather than a title. It is the name of the Savior who belongs not only to Israel but to all nations.

Paul's favorite name for the Savior is **Ho Kyrios** the Lord, which occurs two hundred twenty-two times in his letters. In the Gospels Jesus refers to himself as

22

Kyrios (Aramaic **Mari**) (Mark 11:3, Matthew 7:21, John 13:13). After Jesus' exaltation the term took on a deeper connotation in the worship of the Aramaic-speaking church. In 1 Corinthians 16:22 Paul preserves the title in Aramaic, **Marana tha**, our Lord, come. It was this title which became translated into Greek as **Ho Kyrios.** It is also significant that in Paul's Bible, the Septuagint, **Ho Kyrios** is the translation of **Adonai**, the Hebrew name for God himself. In applying this highest of names to Jesus, Paul does not mean that Jesus has now taken the place of God but that "the light of the knowledge of the glory of God shines from the face of Christ" (2 Corinthians 4:6). "In him the whole fulness of deity dwells bodily" (Colossians 2:9). He is not only the revealer and agent of God's redemptive plan for mankind but it is only through him that the structure of the whole universe becomes known: "He is the image of the invisible God, the first-born of all creation; for in him all things were created, in heaven and on earth, visible and invisible, whether thrones or dominions or principalities or authorities — all things were created through him and for him. He is before all things, and in him all things hold together" (Colossians 1:15-17).

No one in our day has captured so well and expressed so eloquently this Pauline vision as the scientist-theologian Teilhard de Chardin. The universe to him is an evolution moving toward spirit. This spirit is the personal God revealed in the cosmic Christ. In him God invests himself with the majesty of his creation and he is the ultimate consummation of the cosmic process. The sacramental presence of the incarnate God is the radiating and energizing force which will ultimately permeate the whole of creation. Hence the prayer, "Show yourself to us, O Jesus, as the Mighty, the Radiant, the Risen! And so that we should triumph over the world with you, come to us clothed in the glory of the world." [6]

Paul's basic theology, his concepts of grace, redemption, and salvation, must be studied in this profound cosmic setting, not in terms of any narrow subjective analysis. Whatever else we discover in his teaching, it must all be related to his central purpose, to glorify Jesus as Christ and Lord.

CHAPTER TWO

Grace, Salvation, and Redemption

To be a Christian, says Emil Brunner, is to share something which has happened, which is happening, and which will happen. Archibald Hunter, in his book **The Gospel According to St. Paul,** makes good use of this approach and it provides a helpful scheme for our study of Paul's basic theology of salvation by grace. First is salvation as a past event, in which the accent falls on redemption as a once-for-all divine act which has already occurred. Second is salvation as a present experience, the response of faith to God's saving grace and the experience of "being in Christ." Third is salvation as a future hope, Paul's Eschchatological Outlook.

To Paul salvation is a word with three tenses. "We were saved," he says in Romans 8:24. "We are being saved," he says in 1 Corinthians 15:2. "We shall be saved," he says in Romans 5:9. All three are contained in a key passage which is the epitome of Paul's theology: "Therefore being justified by faith, we have peace with God through our Lord Jesus Christ, through whom also we have obtained access into this grace in which we stand, and rejoice in the hope of the glory of God" (Romans 5:1,2). Salvation has been fully accomplished "through our Lord Jesus Christ," by what he did for us on the cross. By faith we have obtained access into his saving grace and now stand in it, enjoying peace with God. But we look forward in joy and hope to the consummation of salvation in glory.

Grace

In whichever tense Paul speaks of salvation his key word is **charis**, grace. This word occurs eighty-eight times in his Epistles. Its basic meaning is expressed also in other words, such as **agape**, love, Paul's theology is a theology of grace through and through. As James Moffatt puts it, "When the apostle sought to transmit 'the light of the knowledge of the glory of God in the face of Jesus Christ' which had dawned upon him outside Damascus, his good news may be described as a message or proclamation announcing that 'All is of grace, and grace is for all.'[7]

It is with a greeting of grace that Paul begins his letters. With slight variations the greeting is always the same. The fullest form, occurring in Galatians, Corinthians, Romans, and Philippians, is "Grace and peace to you from God our Father and the Lord Jesus Christ." The shortest form is in First Thessalonians, "Grace and peace to you." It was also characteristic of the apostle to close a letter on the grace note. He did not allow any conventional phrase like "farewell" to stand alongside grace, for the emphasis on grace was first and last. Especially significant is the last verse of Second Thessalonians: "I, Paul, write this greeting with my own hand. This is the mark of every letter of mine; it is the way I write. The grace of our Lord Jesus Christ be with you all." Even if it were true, as some critics think, that this is an attempt by some other author to establish the Pauline content of the letter, it only proves that Paul's own emphasis was well known. There are variations also in the greeting with which Paul closes his letters. In Galatians it is "The grace of our Lord Jesus Christ be with your spirit." In Ephesians it is "Grace be with all who love our Lord Jesus Christ with love undying." In Colossians it is a simple "Grace be with you." The fullest form is in Second Corinthians: "The grace of the Lord Jesus Christ and the love of

God and the fellowship of the Holy Spirit be with you all." This apostolic benediction became important in the development of the doctrine of the Trinity and it suggests that the Lord Jesus Christ with his grace is the key to this doctrine.

Paul gave the word **charis** its distinctive Christian meaning, something quite different from its connotation in classical Greek or in its use by Paul's contemporaries. In its original sense **charis** meant beauty, attractiveness or loveliness, that which delights or charms. Homer uses it to describe the beauty of a person or the winsomeness of speech. By an interiorizing process **charis** came to signify that which is attractive in disposition or character, hence favor, good will, graciousness. This use still persists, as when we speak of a gracious hostess or a gracious invitation. The word then came to stand for an objective mark of favor, a boon conferred, a kindness done. Finally **charis**, or its Latin form, **gratia**, was used to describe the response to favor, hence gratitude, thankfulness.

In the Septuagint and in Philo the Hebrew word which comes closest to charis, **chesed**, is translated **eleos**, mercy, not **charis**. Grace means simply to "find favor" in the sense of fortunate treatment of a suppliant in the court of a monarch. Philo uses the word chiefly in the plural, favors or bounties on a natural plane and conditioned by merit. In the imperial inscriptions of the first century the word takes on new potential. It is often preceded by an adjective such as "divine" or "immortal" or "eternal" and designates a royal favor or gift to some community by a Nero or a Caligula. Such usage may have influenced Paul to adopt this word to represent the sovereign self-giving love of God. Furthermore, in the mystery cults the word had taken on still another meaning, namely, potent charm, mystical power. In this sense it often became degraded into magic but it pointed to a higher use, the working of divine power.

Then came Paul, "baptizing the word with new meaning," as Hunter puts it, "and henceforth 'grace' became the twin-sister not of loveliness but love — the love of God for undeserving men."[8] It still stands for favor, but it is undeserved favor, incompatible with merit and inseparably bound with the redeeming sacrifice of Christ on the cross. As James Denney defined it, grace is "the love of God, spontaneous, beautiful, unearned, at work in Jesus Christ for the salvation of sinful men."[9] A more elaborate summary is given by James Moffatt in his classic **Grace in the New Testament.** He points out that the gospel stamps grace with a sense of its own, although the other connotations persist. Here is humble recognition of God in worship and fellowship. Men owe all blessings to the goodness, generosity, and forgiveness of God. This kindness is one of authority and majesty. As creatures we enjoy his free good will. This relationship has a moral character. It presupposes sin and the forgiveness of sin, not just fellowship with a friendly spirit. And it implies that we are under obligation to God, as opposed to the humanistic view that we merely use God for our own ends. Belief in grace withers when Christ is only the leader of human enterprise or incentive to moral aspiration. Grace, in a word, is the royal saving power of God manifested in Christ.[10]

Grace, then, is not just one doctrine among others. It is the all-pervasive spirit of theology, the key to God's entire revelation of himself and of his dealings with men. As such it underlies all fundamental doctrines, predestination, atonement, the sacraments, the church, as well as the Christian life and hope. Grace meant all this to Paul. Our present task is to examine grace as it is related to salvation and redemption.

Salvation

Salvation, **soteria**, means healing and deliverance. The word was used in Paul's time to signify well-being in all its forms, whether of body or soul. For Paul the term stands for what the grace of God, revealed in the cross of Jesus Christ, accomplishes for men. Thus he calls the good news which he proclaimed "the gospel of your salvation" (Ephesians 1:13).

The search for salvation was widespread in the Graeco-Roman world of Paul's day. Moral decay was rampant and neither traditional religion nor the prevailing philosophies could satisfy the longing of serious-minded men for spiritual well-being. The old gods, themselves guilty of gross immorality, were held in ridicule. The final answer which either Stoicism or Epicureanism could offer to disillusioned men was suicide. **The salvation which the Gentiles were seeking** was deliverance from uncertainty and insecurity, from inexorable fate and the fear of death. For the Jews salvation meant deliverance from guilt, from sin which separates men from the holy and righteous God. Paul had a gospel which contained the answer to the longings of both the Jew and of the Gentile. It announced victory over sin and death through the redemptive act of Christ and freedom from fear and insecurity through the restoration of a confident personal relationship to God. It was both a remedy for sin and the power of God for a wholesome life. In Hunter's words, "It included not only what a man must be saved **from** but also what he must be saved **to** — reconciliation and righteousness and life."[11]

Paul's message of salvation is an announcement of an event which has already taken place. Salvation is based on what God has already done. "God shows his love for us," declares the apostle, "in that while we were yet sinners, Christ died for us" (Romans 5:8).

"While we were enemies we were reconciled to God by the death of his Son" (Romans 5:10). With Aulen we may speak of the death and resurrection of Christ as the "Christ-deed" or with Bultmann as the "salvation-occurrence." This deed or occurrence is a once-for-all event of past history but it is more than that. Around the cross revolves God's whole redemptive plan for his creation and as such it has cosmic proportions. "God was in Christ reconciling the world to himself" (2 Corinthians 5:19). As Bonhoeffer insisted, the whole world belongs to Christ for he will not give up what he has so dearly won. "For in him all the fullness of God was pleased to dwell, and through him to reconcile all things, whether on earth or in heaven, making peace by the blood of his cross" (Colossians 1:19). Thus Karl Heim can describe Christ as the **Weltvollender**, world-fulfiller. Redemption has already been accomplished by his death and resurrection, the power of a new creation is already at work in the world, and the final triumph of Christ is inevitable. And Oscar Cullmann can speak of the salvation-occurrence as the D-Day when the back of the enemy was broken and of the final victory of V-Day which is therefore sure to come.

Atonement

Paul's doctrine of the atonement is a rich and many-sided complex of ideas, expressed by such terms as reconciliation, justification, expiation, sacrifice, and redemption. Reconciliation and justification imply primarily the restoration of a personal fellowship with God and may therefore be examined in the context of the response of faith to the Christ-deed. Expiatory sacrifice and redemption, on the other hand, point to the Christ-deed itself, to salvation as an objective accomplished fact.

Expiatory sacrifice is the main line of Paul's interpretation of the meaning of the cross. Thus it also

30

dominates subsequent theology of the atonement which follows him. Paul proclaims "the redemption that is in Christ Jesus, whom God put forward as an expiation by his blood" (Romans 3:24-25). "One died for all" (2 Corinthians 5:14). "Christ redeemed us from the curse of the law, having become a curse for us" (Galatians 3:13). "For our sake he made him to be sin who knew no sin, so that in him we might become the righteousness of God" (2 Corinthians 5:21). "For God has done what the law . . . could not do, sending his own Son in the likeness of sinful flesh and for sin . . . (that is, as a sin-offering) (Romans 8:3).

This proclamation of the vicarious and substitutionary character of the death of Christ recognizes the gravity of sin as guilt which must be expiated and the immeasurable depth of the divine love revealed in the atoning sacrifice on the cross. It is faithfully retained by Anselm in terms of feudal justice and by the Reformers in terms of a conciliation between God's righteousness and God's love. Quite a different line of thought is followed by many liberal theologians beginning with Schleiermacher. Jesus is viewed as a uniquely God-conscious and God-dependent man and his death is regarded as the result of his unswerving faithfulness to his vocation as revealer of divine love. This is the way my own teacher, Albert Knudson, a leading personalistic philosopher, interpreted the death of Christ. Here the basic Pauline text is Philippians 2:8 where the crucified Christ is described as "obedient unto death, even death on the cross." This interpretation is true so far as it goes, but it forgets that the vocation to which Jesus was faithful unto death was not only to reveal God but to reconcile men with God. It disregards the context of Paul's reference to the obedient Christ, that he is sovereign Lord, co-equal with God, who assumed the form of a servant to carry out God's redeeming purpose for mankind. His death was not merely that of a man who remained good even though it cost him his life but that of a Mediator who was "delivered up according to the definite plan and foreknowledge of God" (Acts 2:23). Because of the superficial view of sin on which this view rests, it transforms the Mediator into a martyr.

The roots of Paul's concept of expiatory sacrifice lie deep in the Old Testament. To expiate means to annul or neutralize that in man which makes him unfit for communion with God. Through the law which God gave to his people he reveals not only his holy will but also the distance which separates sinful man from him. Thus already at Sinai, where God establishes a covenant with Israel on the basis of the law, Moses sprinkles the "blood of the covenant" upon the people to symbolize the expiation needed when the law is violated. Through the whole sacrificial system Israel is constantly reminded that without the shedding of blood there is no salvation. The symbolism rises to its climax in the annual Day of Atonement when the high priest entered the holiest of the holies and sprinkled the blood of the sacrificial animal upon the **kapporeth**, the mercy seat, the lid of the ark of the covenant, in which the tablets of the law were kept. It is significant that when Paul speaks of "expiation by his blood" the word which he uses for expiation, **hilasterion**, is the same word with which the Septuagint translates **kapporeth**, mercy seat. For Paul the mercy seat is the symbol of the cross of Christ, the center of God's mercy and forgiveness. The symbolism is contained also in **kippur**, the Hebrew word for atonement. It has the literal meaning of **covering** and implies the interposing of the innocent sacrificial victim between the righteous wrath of God and the offender. Prophecy at its highest level presents the Messiah as the vicarious sacrifice, the lamb led to slaughter. The apostolic proclamation applies to Jesus the prophetic word, "He was

32

wounded for our transgressions . . . upon him was the chastisement that made us whole . . . the Lord has laid on him the iniquity of us all" (Isaiah 53).

It is only against this background that we understand Paul's message of the salvation accomplished on the hill of the cross. "Christ died for our sins according to the scriptures" (1 Corinthians 15:3). "He was delivered up for our trespasses" (Romans 4:25). "For our sake he made him to be sin who knew no sin" (2 Corinthians 5:21).

Redemption

Alongside expiatory sacrifice is another strong line of Pauline thought on salvation as an accomplished fact. It is represented by the word **apolytrosis**, redemption. "In him we have redemption through his blood" (Ephesians 1:7). "In whom we have redemption, the forgiveness of sins" (Colossians 1:14). "The redemption which is in Christ Jesus" (Romans 3:24). "Christ redeemed us from the curse of the law" (Galatians 3:13). "You have been set free from sin" (Romans 6:22). "He has delivered us from the dominion of darkness" (Colossians 1:13). "You were bought with a price" (1 Corinthians 6:20).

The word **apolytrosis**, in the sense of deliverance or emancipation, comes from the slave market. The people to whom Paul wrote were familiar with slavery and with the purchase of freedom for a slave. Paul's use of the metaphor of redeeming appears to have special reference to the custom of "sacral manumission," emancipation through the fictitious purchase of a slave by a deity. The owner accompanied the slave to a temple and sold him to a god. In return he received from the temple treasury the purchase-money, **lytron**, which had previously been paid by the slave out of his own earnings. The slave thus became a free man but now he also became the property of the god. It is not difficult to see how such a transaction could be used by Paul to symbolize "the redemption which is in Christ Jesus," although the **lytron** is not our own silver or gold but "the precious blood of Christ." By his death we have been set free from the slavery of sin, from servitude to the yoke of the law, from bondage to the demonic powers of evil. Yet we are not our own. We belong to Christ.

But Paul could also draw upon his own religious heritage for his interpretation of the salvation-occurrence as deliverance. As a "Hebrew of the Hebrews" he could not forget the first great deliverance of God's people, the deliverance from Egyptian bondage. And when he spoke of the blood of Christ as ransom, he was echoing the Lord's own saying, "The Son of Man came to give his life as a ransom for many" (Mark 10:45). Paul couples the deliverance accomplished by the death of Christ with the affirmation of victory over the cosmic "principalities and powers," "the spiritual hosts of wickedness in the heavenly places," "the rulers of this world" which held mankind captive. Paul holds these evil powers responsible for the crucifixion of the King of glory (1 Corinthians 2:8). Christ defeated them through the cross (Colossians 2:15). His victory will be complete when "Christ delivers the kingdom of God to the Father after destroying every rule and every authority and power" (1 Corinthians 15:24).

Paul's interpretation of the atonement in terms of ransom and victory is in the foreground in the Greek fathers, while western thought, patterned on Augustine and Anselm, came to stress guilt and sacrifice. While Luther was not an Augustinian monk for nothing, he also gave full recognition to the other aspect of Pauline thought. "Redemption" was a word dear to him. No one has stated its meaning more beautifully than he does in the explanation of the

Second Article of the Creed: "I believe that Jesus Christ . . . is my Lord, who has redeemed me, a lost and condemned creature, purchased and won me from all sins, from death, and from the power of the devil; not with gold or silver, but with his holy, precious blood and with his innocent suffering and death, that I may be his own, and live under him in his kingdom, and serve him . . ." Luther portrays sin, death, the devil, the law, and the wrath of God as "tyrants" overthrown by Christ. In our day Aulen has contended that the ideas of ransom and victory represent the church's primary approach to the work of Christ. They show God to be the subject as well as the object in the act of atonement, present Christ's whole life of active obedience to God in inseparable unity with the event of his death, and stress the positive and constructive results of Christ's triumph. Even the element of truth in the Abelardian "moral influence" theory of the atonement is thus included.

For Paul the point of view of redemption supplements but does not supplant that of vicarious sacrifice. One-sided emphasis upon the latter can easily lead to pre-occupation with impersonal juridic categories, while the idea of redemption as such does not provide adequate insight either into man's guilt or God's righteousness. Christ's death for sinners reveals how fellowship between God and man can be established without minimizing either the deadly seriousness of sin or the sovereign righteousness of God. Here the substitutionary view shows greater depth than the view which concentrates on Christ as the mighty Conqueror who breaks down the strongholds of evil and sets the captives free. Sinners need not only to be delivered from bondage to the powers of evil but also to be reconciled with the God against whom they have sinned. Charles Wesley brings out the point well: "He breaks the power of **cancelled** sin, he sets the prisoner free." Unless the guilt of sin is cancelled, there can be no true deliverance. Priority must therefore be given to the view that stresses with Paul the primacy of grace: "While we were yet sinners, Christ died for us." The basis of redemption is God's own unique act in which through the sacrifice made on the cross he himself removed the barrier erected by sin and opened for us the way to fellowship with him. The grace of forgiveness becomes ours through faith, but it exists before faith and makes faith possible.

We have discussed salvation as an accomplished fact in terms of Paul's theology of the cross. But we must not forget that for Paul the cross is never to be isolated from the resurrection. Christ "was delivered up for our trespasses and raised for our justification" (Romans 4:25). "If Christ was not raised, then our gospel is null and void, and so is your faith; and we turn out to be lying witnesses for God . . . If Christ was not raised, your faith has nothing in it and you are still in your old state of sin. It follows also that those who have died within Christ's fellowship are utterly lost" (1 Corinthians 15:14 ff., New English Bible).

The resurrection is thus the living center of Paul's theology. It validates and vitalizes everything that Paul teaches about Christ and his work. Without a living Christ Paul would have had no message and no mission. The resurrection distinguishes Christ from all prophets, heroes of faith, founders of religions: "He was designated Son of God in power . . . by his resurrection from the dead" (Romans 1:4). The gospel is "the power of God unto salvation" because it is "the working of his great might which he accomplished in Christ when he raised him from the dead" (Ephesians 1:19-20). It is by this resurrection power that the church lives and carries out its mission. Its sacraments are actual communion with the living Lord. Its members "taste of the powers of the world to come" as they "rise with Christ into a newness of Life." Because the risen Christ is a living reality, the forgiveness of sins, the power for a new life, and victory over death become living realities. Thus to know the meaning of salvation in any of its aspects is to "know the power of his resurrection" (Philippians 3:10).

CHAPTER THREE

Justification and Reconciliation

Two fundamental and interrelated concepts in Paul's message of salvation are justification and reconciliation. When the apostle speaks of salvation in terms of vicarious sacrifice and redemption, he is describing salvation as a purely objective salvation-occurrence. The saving sacrifice has already been made. The redemptive deed has already been done. The victory over the forces of evil has already been won. Justification and reconciliation, on the other hand, show how what Christ has done can become for us the ground for a changed relationship to God, how we can appropriate for ourselves the fruits of Christ's victory.

It would be wrong, however, to regard either justification or reconciliation as merely subjective. To speak of justification by faith is misleading if our faith is considered to be the agency or condition of salvation. Justification is by grace. "They are justified by his grace as a gift" (Romans 3:24). In Bultmann's words, "Not merely salvation is the gift of God but even the condition for it is already the gift of God himself."[12] And the righteousness which justification involves is not an ethical quality in man but his relation to God. Justification is God's own action in rightwising this relation, thus making fellowship with him possible. Faith is surrender to the grace of God, accepting and living by what God gives. So it is also with reconciliation. The exhortation "Be reconciled to God" (2 Corinthians 5:20) rests on the proclamation "while we were yet enemies we were reconciled to God" (Romans 5:10). The exhortation is an invitation to faith, to receive subjectively the objective factual situation brought about by God's action.

Whether we examine salvation as a human experience from the point of view of justification, the acquittal of one who stands condemned before the judgment throne of God, or from the point of view of reconciliation, the restoration to personal fellowship with God, we must have in mind Paul's diagnosis of the human predicament. This he performs in terms of sin, the flesh, and the law.

Sin

According to Paul, I need redemption because I am "sold under sin" (Romans 7:14). I need deliverance because I am a "slave of sin" (Romans 6:17). I am "captive to the law of sin" (Romans 7:23). Sin, for Paul, is not merely an incident of moral failure or a series of wrong choices. It is a basic life-orientation just as faith is. "Whatever does not proceed from faith is sin" (Romans 14:23). Man not only commits this or that sinful act. He is a sinner, an enemy of God, a rebel against his rule. Sin involves the whole man, not just some aspects of his behavior or some side of his nature. Sinful acts are inseparable from the sinner himself. They have their source in the radical wrongness of his relation to God. Paul would have rejected emphatically the shallow popular idea that God hates sin but loves the sinner. It is the sinner himself, not some detachable act of his, that is under the wrath of God. God's wrath is not rage or bad temper but God's holy love reacting against evil. Luther found comfort in the idea of God's wrath, for it shows that God is concerned about me and I can experience this concern as love when my relation to him is set right. Sin leads with inner necessity to death: "If you live according to the flesh you will die" (Romans 8:13). The sinner "deserves to die" (Romans 1:32). The wages which sin pays to its slave is death (Romans 6:16, 23).

For Paul, sin is both endemic and universal. It is a destructive power which dwells within a man and compels him to do what he knows is wrong (Romans 7:15 ff.). This is true of all men, for they are all members of a fallen and sin-tainted race. The apostle is thus led to speak of Adam's fall, for all mankind is one flesh with Adam and his disobedience has affected all. But he does not proceed to describe the fall as an historical event but as a diagnosis of a universal and perrennial human predicament. The key-passage is Romans 5:12: "Sin came into the world through one man and death through sin," but the apostle hastens to add "because all men sinned," not, as Jerome in the Vulgate translated this passage, "**in whom** all men sinned." Luther was the first to detect Jerome's error in translating the apostle's **eph ho** as if it were **en ho** and to give the correct translation, "**dieweil** sie alle gesündiget haben." While affirming the universality of sin, the apostle does not permit us to escape responsibility by tracing sin by biological necessity to a corrupt Adamic nature. Those who echo the New England Primer's "In Adam's fall we sinned all" are on the wrong track. Of his own will, without external compulsion, each of us falls into sin. Paul's ultimate answer to the question of the origin of sin is to affirm "the mystery of iniquity," which is philosophically expressed by Kierkegaard, "Sin posits itself" and "Guilt is the most concrete expression of existence."

Flesh

The tool which sin uses is the flesh, **sarx**, a word which is found ninety times in Paul's letters and has various shades of meaning. Basically it is the equivalent of the Hebrew word **basar**, the material side of man's nature which ties him up with "all flesh," the whole bundle of created life. **Sarx** must be distinguished from **soma**, the body, the concrete, individual human being marked off from other men and the rest of nature by his physical structure. At times Paul uses **sarx** in a morally neutral sense to denote natural earthly human existence in its solidarity and its weakness and mortality over against God. It is simply leading one's life as a human. Thus it is used even to describe Christ's humanness, as in John 1:14, "The word became flesh." But since human existence apart from the redeeming work of Christ is sinful alienation from the Creator, flesh also designates the distance between man and God. Flesh is not intrinsically evil, but it is corrupted by sin and becomes the base of operations for sin, for it gives sin its opportunity (Romans 7:11; Galatians 5:13). Natural human frailty opens the door to sin. To live "after the flesh" [**kata sarka**] is not primarily to live sensuously but to live godlessly, in sinful self-reliance. Thus such sins as idolatry and jealousy are not rooted in man's physical structure, but they are nevertheless "works of the flesh," for they are the results of estrangement from God. Living "after the flesh" is turning away from the Creator, finding one's security in the created world and putting one's trust in his own human strength. Flesh, for Paul, as Karl Barth puts it, "stands for the complete inadequacy of the creature before his Creator." The opposite of living according to the flesh is "living by the Spirit." "To set the mind on the flesh is death, but to set the mind on the Spirit is life and peace" (Romans 8:6).

Law

Man needs to be delivered not only from bondage to sin and the flesh but also from the yoke of the law. The law is the Torah, interpreted not only as the law of Moses governing Israel but as the universal revelation of God's will for human life. As such "The law is holy, and the commandment is holy, just and good" (Romans 7:12). Why, then, does Paul speak about the "curse of the law"? Because the human predicament is such that the law which was intended to give life actually leads to sin and death. "Through the law comes knowledge of sin," says Paul (Romans 3:20). Bultmann points out convincingly, "This sentence does not mean that through the Law man is led to knowledge of what sin is but does mean that by it he is led into sinning."[13] Far from being an incentive to do God's will, the law "revives sin" (Romans 7:9) and "increases the trespass" (Romans 5:20). As an example, Paul says, the commandment "You shall not covet" only "wrought in me all kinds of covetousness" (Romans 7:8). Human nature is such that the fruit of the forbidden tree tastes sweetest.

In the sharp contrast which Paul draws between law and grace, law has a purely negative function. "Why the law?" he asks, and answers, "because of transgressions," not only to bring transgressions to light but to provoke transgressions. And since the result of transgression is death, the ultimate purpose of the law is to lead to death. "The letter (that is, the law) **kills**" (2 Corinthians 3:6). "When the commandment came sin revived and I died; the very commandment which promised life proved to be death to me" (Romans 7:9-10). "If a law had been given which could make alive, then righteousness would indeed be by the law" (Galatians 3:21). The law may promise life but it yields only death. Life and righteousness are ours only through faith in Christ.

But does not Paul ascribe to the law the positive function of preparing us to receive Christ, when he describes the law as a **paidagogos eis Christon**, a tutor and guardian leading us to Christ? (Galatians 3:23-26) Yes, the law does this, but not in the direct sense of training us for grace but only in the indirect sense of leading us to an impasse from which only Christ can deliver us. "Through the commandment" sin "becomes sinful beyond measure" (Romans 7:13). "Law came in to increase the trespass, but where sin increased, grace abounded all the more" (Romans 5:20). The word for "came in" [pareiserchomai] means literally "To come in by stealth" or "to slip in between." The trespass has broken the direct personal relation to God, and the law spells out this tragic situation, even aggravating it. The very fact that God's loving will is known as impersonal law shows that something has crept in between man and God. The law which commands man to love God with his whole heart is the clearest indication of the perversion. The fact that love to God is presented as a command and an obligation shows that man no longer exists in the love of God, for genuine love is spontaneous and cannot be commanded or coerced into being. As Kant observed, "A command that one should do something willingly is in itself a contradiction." The more desperately, then, a man tries to fulfil the law of love, the more clearly he discerns his basic maladjustment to God. The law has done its work when it has brought us to the situation where we face an inescapable either-or: either the works of the law or the grace of God in Jesus Christ.

"Do we then overthrow the law by this faith?" asks Paul. The answer is, "By no means! On the contrary, we uphold the law" (Romans 3:31). Paul upholds the law by preserving its true function to expose and aggravate sin, to accuse and condemn the sinner, and to drive him to despair of his effort to earn God's favor by obeying the law. Paul denies the right to moralize the law, to tone down its true character as terrifying agent of divine wrath, to transform it into a gentle guide for holy living, to make it a way of salvation, a rival of the gospel. The law is "holy and just and good," for it is the revelation of the holy will of God, but no man can satisfy its demands. The law demands absolute perfection and pronounces a curse upon "every one who does not abide by all things written in the book of the law and do them" (Galatians 3:10). Not only does man's effort to achieve salvation by keeping the law lead him into sin, but the effort itself is sin. Paul learned this from his own painful experience. It was his zeal for the law that led him into his greatest sin, the persecution of the church of Christ. Paul concludes not only that "a man is not justified by the works of the law" but that according to God's plan of salvation no one **is to be** or **shall be** justified by the works of the law but only by faith in Christ (Galatians 2:16). As Paul Althaus expressed it, it is God's sovereign will to save us by grace alone, not because man is a sinner but because the sinner is a man, and God's way with man is the way of grace.

Man-centered salvation by the works of the law and God-centered salvation by grace are thus mutually exclusive. What a terrific struggle Paul the Pharisee must have undergone before he could confess: the law is not the way of salvation. In the light of the law the zealous Pharisee discovered only the wrongness of his best efforts. He was set right with God when he discovered the grace which justifies the ungodly and which enabled him to say, "Now we are discharged from the law, dead to that which held us captive, so that we serve not under the old written code but in the new life of the Spirit" (Romans 7:6).

Since the law belongs to the old aeon, not to the new, Paul could declare, "Christ is the end of the law" (Romans 10:4). To one who serves "in the new life of the Spirit" the reign of the law has ended. He has entered into a new relation to God which is determined by grace, in which love is the compelling motive. And love is incommensurate with any form of legalism.

Justification

If sin has broken man's filial relation to God, and man cannot repair the break by obeying God's law, how is the restoration of fellowship with God brought about? Paul's answer is the doctrine of justification by faith, set forth in Romans and Galatians. To the Protestant Reformers this doctrine was of such paramount importance that they regarded it as the whole gospel in a nutshell. Modern biblical scholarship has vindicated the Reformers' view as a valid exposition of the gospel. The heart of the Christian message is indeed the setting right of man's relation to God on the basis of the work of Christ. The Reformers also understood correctly the meaning of the Pauline **dikaiousthai**, to justify. It is not correctly translated by the Latin **justificare** in the sense of **justum facere**, to make just. It is a declaration of acquittal for an accused person.

Justification is a forensic term, originating in the law court. It presents a courtroom scene in which the divine Judge, having found the sinner guilty on the basis of his own actions, nevertheless pronounces him to be innocent because the righteousness of Christ, which he has appropriated by faith, is "imputed" to him. To use a kindred metaphor, while an examination of the sinner's ledger reveals him to be morally and spiritually bankrupt, he nevertheless turns out to be solvent, since faith has placed to his credit all that Christ has earned. Justification is, therefore, as the Reformers expressed it, **propter Christum, per fidem**, on account of Christ and through faith.

Such a method of presenting salvation preserves the factual objective character of the gospel and guards the purity of its central content, the free grace of God, unconditioned by anything men do. But preoccupation with the forensic interpretation has its dangers too. If the seventeenth century Protestant orthodoxists were telling the whole truth in insisting that justification does not deal with man at all but only with the relation between man and God and that it takes place not in the human heart but in the judgment hall of God, then the question how God's saving grace becomes ours is left unanswered. Man becomes a mere spectator of a divine drama without any actual encounter with God. Paul avoids this danger by using justification to signify not merely impersonal acquittal but also personal forgiveness and pardon. Thus in Romans 4, in the very context in which he speaks of the God who "justifies the ungodly" and of the faith that is "reckoned as righteousness," he quotes Psalms 32: "Blessed are those whose iniquities are forgiven, and whose sins are covered, blessed is the man against whom the Lord will not reckon his sin." Paul's key-phrase "the righteousness of God" is not a static divine attribute but a divine activity, "God's way of righting wrong," as the New English Bible translates the phrase. Justification is God's gracious way of setting man right with himself by forgiving his sins.

The emphasis on forgiveness, over against a purely forensic interpretation, is strong in Luther. "Justice," he says in his **Lectures on Romans**, "is used in Scripture in a vastly different sense from its use by the philosophers and jurists."[14] He goes on to explain that righteousness in its Pauline usage is not the righteousness of the law courts but a redeeming and transforming righteousness. In a later sermon he declares, "Note this fact carefully, that when you find in the Scriptures the word **God's Justice** . . . it means the revealed grace and mercy of God through Jesus Christ."[15] John Wesley has the same interpretation: "The plain scriptural notion of justification is pardon, the forgiveness of sins."[16] Joachim Jeremias, contemporary New Testament scholar, states emphatically: "Justification is forgiveness, nothing but forgiveness, for Christ's sake."[17] Thus what Paul means by "justifying the ungodly" may be expressed more effectively by the language of the home rather than that of the law court, as our Lord does in his parable of the prodigal son. And Paul's own analogy of dying and rising with Christ is a more powerful figure of speech than acquittal in court for expressing the entrance into the new life. In any case, if justification is the article by which the church stands or falls, as the Reformers thought, its meaning cannot be restricted to the original forensic connotation. Paul never separates justification from the new relation to God and the power for a new life which it bestows.

The doctrine of justification derives its fundamental importance from the fact that it gives powerful expression to the whole new way of salvation which Paul had discovered, the way of the gospel as opposed to the way of the law. Gospel, grace, and faith are correlative terms describing God himself in saving action. They are the antitheses of law, works, and merit. Justification is the sovereign and merciful act of God in accepting with favor the sinner who admits his own utter inability to be anything but a sinner and therefore thankfully accepts fellowship with God as a totally undeserved gift. This is Paul's message of justification by grace. But to accept God's grace in faith does not mean to find a way to avoid God's judgment throne. It means to find a way to meet judgment. Because God's standard of judgment is his own grace, not the law, he accepts with favor the sinner who entrusts himself to grace, even though he stands condemned by the law. God thus comes to man both as judge and as rescuer. He brings man's proudest achievements under his judgment and exposes the pathetic meaninglessness of his God-estranged existence. But the wonder of his grace is that his saving love encompasses man in the midst of the estrangement. He justifies the ungodly.

He acquits the guilty. He receives the sinner into fellowship with himself, for he has it in his heart to love sinners as they are. Such is the light of the knowledge of God that radiates from Jesus Christ.

This is the good news which Paul proclaimed and which Luther described as the true treasure of the church in all ages. It led the Reformer to portray God as "nothing but an abyss of love." And it inspired James Denney to wish that he could enter every church in Scotland and, holding a crucifix before the congregation, shout, "God loves like that!"

Reconciliation

Justification may be the gospel in a nutshell, but no one word can bear the full weight of Paul's impassioned exposition of the grace which sets men right with God. Another rich word is reconciliation. Paul uses the Greek noun **katallage** and the verb **katallasso** or **apokatallasso** or **katallagenai**. The meaning is the same as the English word of Latin derivation, reconciliation, the restoration or healing of broken personal relations. The basic texts are: Romans 5:10-11: "For if while we are enemies we were reconciled to God by the death of his Son, much more, now that we are reconciled, shall we be saved by his life. Not only so, but we also rejoice in God through our Lord Jesus Christ, through whom we have now received our reconciliation." 2 Corinthians 5:18-20: "All this is from God, who through Christ reconciled us to himself and gave us the ministry of reconciliation; that is, God was in Christ reconciling the world to himself, not counting their trespasses against them, and entrusting to us the message of reconciliation. . . We beseech you on behalf of Christ, be reconciled to God." Ephesians 2:14-16: "For he is our peace, who has made us both one, and has broken down the dividing wall of hostility . . . that he

48

might create in himself one new man in place of the two, so making peace, and might reconcile us both to God in one body through the cross, thereby bringing the hostility to an end." Colossians 1:19-20: "For in him all the fullness of God was pleased to dwell, and through him to reconcile to himself all things, whether on earth or in heaven, making peace by the blood of his cross."

Paul uses interchangeably the terms justification and reconciliation. Thus in Romans 5 he says in verse 9 "we are justified" and in verse 10 "we are reconciled." Both describe God in saving action, but in reconciliation this is stated specifically in terms of personal relations rather than in the language of the law court. Reconciliation also expresses more clearly that the release is not only from guilt, the curse of sin, but also from sinning, from the power of sin.

Sin destroys the fellowship with God for which man was created and brings about the need for reconciliation. Paul uses a variety of powerful figures of speech to describe the restoration of fellowship effected by the cross of Christ. Between man and God is a barrier, the cross removes it. Man stands accused before the judgment throne of God, the cross acquits him. Man is an enemy of God, the cross brings peace. Man is a slave, the cross buys his freedom. Man is hopelessly in debt, the cross pays his debt and releases him from the debtor's prison. Man has lost his filial status and becomes an alien to God his father. The cross restores him to God's family circle by bringing about adoption as a child of God.

Paul never raises the question, "How is God to be reconciled?" The idea common in world religions that man must do something to propitiate or appease God is entirely foreign to him. It is man, not God, who needs to be reconciled. God is always the subject, never the object, of reconciliation. "All this is from God, who through Christ reconciled us to himself" (2

Corinthians 5:18). "While we were enemies we were reconciled to God" (Romans 5:10). "While we were yet helpless, at the right time Christ died for the ungodly" (Romans 5:6). The reconciling deed was done without any effort or even knowledge on man's part. The barrier has been removed and a new objective situation has been brought about which makes possible the restoration of fellowship. All man can do is to receive the accomplished reconciliation.

To this end God has set up the "ministry" or "message" of reconciliation through which men are invited to accept in faith what God has done. Reconciliation thus sounds clearly the note of grace, man's complete dependence on God's own saving action. The emphasis is on the objective nature of this action. The enmity which the cross overcomes is not man's subjective feeling of hostility or resentment toward God but the total human predicament of rebellion against God. And the restoration involves not only individual men and mankind as a whole but "all things, whether on earth or in heaven." Reconciliation is nothing less than cosmic in scope. The Reconciler is the cosmic Christ who makes cosmic peace through a cosmic cross.

It is erroneous, then, to interpret the ministry or message of reconciliation as human strategy for bringing peace. But the cosmic event does reveal God's strategy for restoring broken personal relations both between God and man and man and man. Paul weaves both aspects together when he tells the Ephesians that the Christ who abolished the enmity between God and man also broke down the dividing wall of hostility between Jew and Gentile, reconciling "both to God in one body through the cross" (Ephesians 2:14-16). The cross reveals God's way of bringing reconciliation, of healing rifts, or making peace. When a rift has occurred in human relations, each party waits for the other to make the first move toward reconciliation, and the rift only gets deeper. If it is to be healed, the one or the other must take the initiative, go half-way and then more than half-way. What God has done, proclaims Paul, is to go all the way in freely given uncalculating love to heal the rift of our sin and to draw us to himself. And the same agape-love is the motivating power in the lives of the reconciled.

Whether Paul speaks of justification or of reconciliation, he is speaking of God's grace, or salvation as God's gift. But man is not saved unless he makes God's gift his own. The word which Paul uses for this subjective aspect of salvation is "faith." What Paul means by "faith" is the appropriate starting-point for the next topic of our study, salvation as the experience of one who takes what God gives and lives by it.

CHAPTER FOUR

Salvation as Personal Experience

Thus far we have studied Paul's doctrine of salvation in objective terms. Salvation is the work of divine grace, centering in the atoning death of Christ on the cross and bringing about a change in the relation of mankind to God, a change described as redemption, justification, and reconciliation. We turn now to the subjective and personal aspect of salvation, to Paul's answer to the question, "What must I do to be saved?"

Faith

When this question was asked by the Philippian jailer, Paul replied, "**Believe** in the Lord Jesus, and you will be saved" (Acts 16:31). The word for personal acceptance of the salvation accomplished in the Christ-deed is **faith**. This word occurs as noun or verb, **pistis** or **pisteuo**, some 200 times in Paul's letters, and is rich in meaning.

Faith stands, first of all, for **receptivity**, for openness to the gospel and acceptance of the salvation which it offers. It is in faith that the gospel finds its fruition. In this sense Paul can use faith as a synonym for the gospel, as when he speaks of "preaching the faith" (Galatians 1:23) and of "the word of faith which we preach" (Romans 10:8). When the response to the gospel is whole-hearted commitment, man is set right with God. "For man believes with his heart and so is justified" (Romans 10:10). Faith is not an accomplishment of any kind but simply taking God at his word when he offers salvation as a gift. It is that childlike receptivity, spiritual poverty, acute concern, hunger and thirst after righteousness, which Jesus in the beatitudes makes the one entrance requirement into the Kingdom. This is the attitude which opened the door to paradise to the thief on the cross and which led the Philippian jailer from the verge of suicide to midnight baptism.

Faith is not only receptivity but also **confession**. "If you confess with your lips that Jesus is Lord and believe in your heart that God raised him from the dead, you will be saved" (Romans 10:9). Faith is not a nebulous disposition of piety. It is "faith in;" it always has a specific object, God in Christ. It is directed not to a proposition but to a person. The apostolic church was right in representing Paul as saying, "I know **whom** (not **what**) I have believed" (2 Timothy 1:12). Paul's usual reference is to Jesus Christ as the object of faith, but there is no difference in meaning when he speaks of faith in God, for God is in Christ, or of faith in the gospel, for Christ is the heart of the gospel.

Since faith arises from "what is heard" in the gospel (Romans 10:17), it contains definite **knowledge**. It is the "light of the knowledge of the glory of God in the face of Christ" (2 Corinthians 4:6). Faith is anchored in the factual truth of the kerygma, the validity of the resurrection and the lordship of the risen Christ. But the knowledge of faith is not a knowledge of impersonal facts, however important, but a knowledge of the heart. Thus Paul speaks of the "surpassing worth of knowing Christ Jesus" and prays "that I may know him and the power of his resurrection" (Philippians 3:8-10). To use two German words for "to know," through faith a man comes to know Christ in the sense of **kennen**, not that of **wissen**. He does not merely become acquainted with and accept as true what the gospel says about him, but enters into a personal fellowship with him which transforms his entire existence.

The basic Pauline meaning of faith is **trust**. As a concrete example of trust Paul presents Abraham. Abraham trusted in God to make good his promise that Abraham would become the father of many nations. "He did not weaken in faith," says Paul, "when he considered his own body, which was as good as dead because he was about a hundred years old, or when he considered the barrenness of Sarah's womb. No distrust made him waver concerning the promise of God, but he grew strong in his faith as he gave glory to God, fully convinced that God was able to do what he had promised. That is why his faith was 'reckoned to him as righteousness' " (Romans 4:19-22). Paul concludes that faith brings about the new rightwising with God for everyone who "trusts him who justifies the ungodly" (4:5).

Along with receptivity, confession, knowledge, and trust, Paul understands faith as **obedience**. The purpose of his apostleship, he says, is to produce a **hypakoe pisteos**, the obedience of faith. (Romans 1:5). The acceptance of the gospel in faith is an act of obedience whereby, like Abraham, one surrenders his own will to the will of God. Thus Paul describes faith as "obedience in acknowledging the gospel of Christ" (2 Corinthians 9:13) and accuses the Jews who have not come to faith of disobedience to the gospel (Romans 10:16). The believer "takes every thought captive to obey Christ" (2 Corinthians 10:5). He is a new man who has accepted a new Lord and under him a new life in responsibility to him.

As the principle of salvation, faith is radically opposed to "works," to every attempt on man's part to earn salvation by his good deeds. Salvation by grace is the direct antithesis of the works of the law. Those who seek to be justified by obeying the law, says Paul, "are severed from Christ" and "have fallen away from grace" (Galatians 5:4). Saving righteousness "depends on faith, in order that the promise may rest on grace" (Romans 4:16). This is Paul's recurrent emphasis as he expounds God's way of salvation in opposition to human religiosity. "I do not nullify the grace of God, for if justification were through the law, then Christ died to no purpose" (Galatians 2:21). "For Christ is the end of the law, that every one who has faith may be justified" (Romans 10:4). Accepting in faith what God has done in Christ puts an end to all boasting of human achievement. "Then what becomes of boasting? It is excluded. On what principle? On the principle of works? No, but on the principle of faith" (Romans 3:27).

Although Paul is firm in rejecting good works as a condition of salvation, he is just as firm in demanding them as a consequence of salvation. Faith is a sham unless it issues in works of love. True faith is "faith working through love" (Galatians 5:6). Since faith is founded upon grace, God's own love, the faith that works through love may itself be called grace. Thus Paul speaks "about the grace of God which has been shown in the churches of Macedonia," as they gave with overflowing liberality to the relief of the saints, and concludes, "God is able to make every grace abound in you, so that you may always have enough of everything and may provide in abundance for every good work" (2 Corinthians 8:1; 9:8). As Nygren points out, for Paul the agape which characterizes the activity of faith is God's own love operating in believers.

Finally, for Paul, faith is not only an act of decision and commitment with which Christian life begins but also a continuing life-attitude. "The life I now live in the flesh," he says, "I live by faith in the Son of God who loved me and gave himself for me" (Galatians 2:20). Faith is the God-centered life-attitude just as sin is the self-centered life-attitude. Thus "whatever does not proceed from faith is sin" (Romans 14:23). As Luther expressed it, faith is the wedding ring which establishes a life-union of **ich dein und du mein** between a believer and his Savior. And in committing him to vital communion with Christ it also unites him with the communion of all believers, the body of Christ, the church.

Life in Faith

Paul's description of faith as a life-attitude leads us from an analysis of the structure of faith to an examination of life in faith. Here we come most directly to grips with the Pauline doctrine that salvation is a present and on-going reality, that we not only have been saved but also are being saved. Salvation is a once-for-all occurrence in the past and it is an experience by which the believer responded in faith to God's grace in Christ. But it is also a continuing process of growth in grace. The traditional theological term for this process is sanctification. Paul describes this aspect of salvation in various ways. Believers have been "delivered from the dominion of darkness" and transferred "to the kingdom of his beloved Son" (Colossians 1:13). They have a new status and level of existence, for they now "stand in grace" (Romans 5:2). They have been admitted into God's family as adopted children (Galatians 4:5; Romans 8:15). The metaphor of adoption stands for the fact that we have become God's children by grace, only Christ being Son by nature. But we are children who are to grow "to mature manhood, to the measure of the stature of the fullness of Christ" (Ephesians 4:13).

The strongest of the Pauline words for existence as Christians is **life**, life in its richest and fullest meaning. "He who through faith is righteous shall live (Romans 1:17). "The free gift of God is eternal life in Christ Jesus our Lord" (Romans 6:23). "Christ died for us that whether we wake or sleep, we should live together with him" (1 Thessalonians 5:10). The new life of the believer is so thoroughly determined by the basic salvation-occurrence that Paul can speak of it as a duplication of the crucifixion and resurrection of Christ. "We know that our old self was crucified with him so that the sinful body might be destroyed, and we might no longer be enslaved to sin" (Romans 6:6). "Those who belong to Christ Jesus have crucified the flesh with its passions and desires" (Galatians 5:24). "I have been crucified with Christ; it is no longer I who live but Christ who lives in me" (Galatians 2:20). By the cross of Christ "the world has been crucified to me and I to the world" (Galatians 6:14). "But if we have died with Christ, we believe that we shall also live with him" (Romans 6:8). "As Christ was raised from the dead by the glory of the Father, we too might walk in newness of life" (Romans 6:4). "You have been raised with Christ . . . for you have died, and your life is hid with Christ in God" (Colossians 3:1-3).

Paul's constant emphasis is on the radical Christ-centeredness of the new life. "Not I but Christ in me." Sanctification, like justification, is a free gift of grace, not man's achievement. Justification and sanctification stand for two inseparable aspects of living faith, justification for the intake, sanctification for the outflow, of divine grace. In justification faith receives the new life in Christ as a gift, in sanctification faith bears the fruit of the new life. In Kierkegaard's language, the life of faith is the life of the open palm. Day by day and moment by moment we receive the new life, empowered by the living Christ, in the open palm of faith. And day by day and moment by moment we give it back to him in works of love, but we never enclose possessing fingers around it as though it were our own.

The problem of the relation of God's activity and man's activity is one which theologians have debated through the centuries. Paul, like other New Testament writers, clearly ascribes all good works to God's activity in man and yet repeatedly exhorts us to do good works. Paul brings the two emphases together in one apparently paradoxical statement: "Work out your own salvation with fear and trembling, for God is at work in you, both to will and to work for his good pleasure" (Philippians 2:12-13). You must work with utmost conscientiousness because God does it all! Moralists from Pelagius on have overstressed the truth contained in the first half of the statement, "Work out your own salvation," often to the point of ignoring the divine factor. Monergists from Augustine on have tended to emphasize the second half, "God is at work in you," so strongly that little room has been left for human responsibility. Synergists have attempted to solve the dilemma in terms of divine-human co-operation in which the activity and the responsibility are ascribed partly to God and partly to man.

Paul makes no such division, nor does he say, "Man must act, although God acts," but "**because God acts.**" The indicative of God's action is the imperative of man's action. Ethelbert Stauffer sums up the Pauline solution in this way: "God's active will summons man's will to action . . . God's action becomes effective in man's. God himself is at work in our work. The grace of God is potential energy which seeks actualization. The Spirit is at one and the same time a gift and a task. Divine election means being called to serve . . . As the power of God's will grows, the effort of man's will does not decrease, but grows."[18] What Paul is saying is that the redeeming will of God to which we owe our salvation realizes itself in consecrated living.

Being in Christ

Paul's usual expression for the life of faith is the phrase "in Christ" or "in the Lord." The **einai en Christo,**

58

(to be in Christ) like **pistis**, occurs some two hundred times in the Pauline epistles. Sometimes it stands simply for "Christian," as when Paul calls Onesimus "a beloved brother . . . both in the flesh and in the Lord," meaning "as a man and as a Christian" (Philemon 16). But "being in Christ" means more than that. One who has been baptized "into Christ" has had his life taken up into Christ's life and lives in intimate communion with him. In Deissmann's words, this phrase describes "the most intimate fellowship imaginable of the Christian with the living spiritual Christ."[19] Deissmann, Bousset, and others regard **einai en Christo** as the key to Paul's whole theology and speak of a "Christ mysticism" which Paul developed under the influences of the Greek mysteries. For Schweitzer, "being in Christ" is indeed Paul's central motif, but this is a unique kind of mysticism, not typically Hellenistic. For Bultmann, Paul represents the Hellenistic church, not the Hellenistic mysteries. To be in Christ, therefore, is not confined to private experience but stands for the basic nature of the Christian life as such, including its eschatological and ecclesiological aspects. "It denotes not . . . an individual mystical relationship to Christ, but the fact that the individual actual life of the believer, living not out of himself but out of the divine deed of salvation, is determined by Christ."[20] Most interpreters today agree that to be in Christ means not only to be "in communion with Christ" but also to be "in the community of Christ" which is his body, the church. As Archibald Hunter puts it, "What Paul has in mind is changed men and women living in a changed society, with Christ the author of the change in the individual, and Christ the living centre of the new environment in which they live."[21]

While Paul's own conversion experience, which gave a new center to his life, is at the root of **einai en Christo**, he uses the phrase to describe various kinds of conduct and attitude. This is not mysticism in the ordinary sense of something solitary, mysterious, ecstatic, or otherworldly. It is "in Christ" or "in the Lord" that Christians not only trust, hope and rejoice but also tell the truth, work, stand firm, agree with one another, have brotherly love, welcome travelers, send greetings, get married, and finally, die. Whatever they do and whatever happens to them bears the stamp of "in Christ," for their whole life at all levels is determined by Christ.

Holy Spirit

To be "in Christ" is synonymous with being "in the Spirit." Paul uses the two phrases interchangeably, as when he parallels "sanctified in Christ Jesus" (1 Corinthians 1:2) with "sanctified in the Holy Spirit" (Romans 15:16) and "Rejoice in the Lord" (Philippians 3:1) with "joy in the Holy Spirit" (Romans 14:17). So indistinguishable in the experience of the believer are the indwelling Christ and the indwelling Spirit that the apostle can say "The Lord is the Spirit" (2 Corinthians 3:17) and "the last Adam (meaning Christ) became a life-giving Spirit" (1 Corinthians 15:45). Paul does not identify the person of the Holy Spirit with the person of Christ. Objectively, as in the apostolic benediction, they are different, but subjectively they are the same. We do not experience the presence of the Holy Spirit instead of the presence of Christ. Without Christ we do not have the Spirit, and without the Spirit we do not have Christ. The Spirit is the earthly presence of the exalted Lord, the resurrection power of Christ at work here and now. Therefore "Anyone who does not have the Spirit of Christ does not belong to him" (Romans 8:9). Hence the decisive importance of Paul's question, "Did you receive the Holy Spirit when you believed?" (Acts 19:2).

The gospel which Paul proclaimed was not a mere communication of ideas but a transmission of the power of the Spirit. "My speech and my preaching," he says, "were not in persuasive words of wisdom but in demonstration of the Spirit and power, that your faith should not stand in the wisdom of men but in the power of God" (1 Corinthians 2:4-5). Faith is essentially the new life, with new insight, courage, and strength, resulting from the rich personal contact with God provided by the Spirit who makes "God in Christ" an experienced reality. The Spirit frees from sin and death (Romans 8:13), brings about a filial relation to God (Romans 8:15-16), intercedes and inspires prayer in the hearts of believers (Romans 8:26-27), provides insight and wisdom (1 Corinthians 2:10-13), and produces the harvest of holiness (Galatians 5:22). Borrowing a term from current commercial usage, Paul describes the Spirit as **arrabon**, meaning down payment or first installment by which the buyer bound himself to complete the full payment. Through the Spirit the believer already tastes of the powers of the world to come and has the pledge and earnest of the salvation to be perfected (2 Corinthians 1:22; 5:5).

Just as being "in Christ" applies to the ordinary everyday life of the Christian in the world, so also being "in the Spirit" is not confined to an inner spiritual realm. Over against all idealistic interpretations, Paul affirms that the Spirit realizes himself in the physical world. Your true "**spiritual** worship," he says, is "to present your **bodies** as a living sacrifice, holy and acceptable to God" (Romans 12:1). Our bodies are the "temple of the Holy Spirit" (1 Corinthians 3:16). The Lord rules in our bodies over our whole existence, not just the inner life. "Do you not know," asks the apostle, "That your bodies are members of Christ? Shall I therefore take the members of Christ and make them members of a prostitute?" "Shun immorality, for it is a defilement of the temple of the Spirit" and "glorify God in your body" (1 Corinthians 6:15 ff.). The same realism characterizes Paul's teaching on the sacraments. In baptism we are united with the body of Christ. And in the Eucharist the Spirit is connected with bodily reality and carries bodily threats and warnings (1 Corinthinas 11:29-30). Finally, the work of the Spirit culminates in the resurrection of the body. "If the Spirit of him who raised Jesus from the dead dwells in you, he who raised Christ Jesus from the dead will give life to your mortal bodies also through his Spirit which dwells in you" (Romans 8:11).

Charismata

In his struggle with the enthusiasts, Paul is led to explore thoroughly the problem of charismata, the special gifts of the Spirit. He gives charisma a precise meaning. It is a gift of the Spirit, over and above the natural gifts and talents which we have on the basis of creation and which we are to offer to God as a living sacrifice. But it is not primarily miracle or ecstasy. It is a special participation of each Christian in the grace given in baptism and in the service to which it energizes. Service in love, with each Christian using his own special gift of grace for the building up of the whole body of Christ, gives the church a harmonious and effective charismatic unity. The charismata are not restricted to a select few. Every Christian is a steward of God's varied grace. Nor does a charisma become a possession of one who receives it. It can be lost if it is not used in the proper way, and it is not properly used if it only promotes an individual's own spirituality. The standard by which charismata are to be evaluated is the edification of the church. "Since you are eager for manifestations of the Spirit, strive to excel in building up the church . . . Let all things be done for edification" (1 Corinthians 14:12, 26).

Surpassing all other charismata is **agape** (1 Corinthians 13). As Hunter expresses it, if Paul "had been compelled to arrange the gifts of the Spirit in order of merit, love would have stood first and 'tongues' last."[22]

Paul's evaluation of the gifts of the Spirit is thus quite different from that of the apostolic community in general. Hermann Gunkel has pointed out the sharp contrast: "The community regards as pneumatic the extraordinary in the life of the Christian, Paul the ordinary; they, that which is peculiar to individuals; Paul, that which is common to all; they, that which occurs abruptly; Paul, that which is constant; they, that which is special in the Christian life; Paul, the Christian life itself. Hence the value which the primitive church attaches to miracles, Paul attaches to being a Christian. No more is that which is individual and sporadic held to be the divine in man; the Christian man as such is the spiritual man."[23]

Paul himself was a "spiritual" with a capacity for profound mystical experience, a "charismatic" who could say, "I speak in tongues more than you all" (1 Corinthians 14:18). But he was reticent about disclosing his private ecstasies (2 Corinthians 12). When he felt compelled to speak about them, he said, "I speak as a fool." He put glossolalia in its place by declaring, "In church I would rather speak five words with my mind, in order to instruct others, than ten thousand words in a tongue" (1 Corinthians 14:19). More important than the special experiences of individuals is the common life in the Spirit, in which all Christians share. More excellent than the unique gifts of prophesying, healing, and speaking in tongues is the love that impels all Christian activity. More vital than a baptism by the Spirit in some past experience is to be filled by the Spirit again and again and continually to be won anew by Christ in order to perform works of love.

The Church

Life "in Christ" and "in the Spirit" is, finally, life "in the church." Paul knows no such person as a solitary Christian, for the Spirit who creates faith in Christ also binds believers together in "The fellowship of the Spirit." The apostle uses vivid and varied imagery in describing the church. It is the "temple of God" (1 Corinthians 3:16), it is the "household of faith," (Galatians 6:10), it is the "bride of Christ" (2 Corinthians 11:2). Two models are of definitive importance — the "people of God" and the "body of Christ."

When Paul calls the church "the **ecclesia** of God" (1 Corinthians 10:32), he is using the word with which the Septuagint translates the Hebrew **qahal**, the gathered people of God. To Paul the church is "the Israel of God" (Galatians 6:16) and "the seed of Abraham" (Galatians 3:29), thus having continuity with the ancient people of God and yet a new creation of the Spirit. In it the old cermonial laws no longer apply and the wall of partition between Jew and Gentile is abolished. All who have faith in Christ, whatever their nation, race, sex, or social status, constitute the true people of God. They are the communion of saints, the community of those whom the Holy Spirit has united with Christ. The New English Bible is right in translating as "people of God" the term **hoi hagioi**, saints, as Paul addresses his readers, for it means simply Christians. These people existed in scattered groups dotting the Roman Empire, and Paul often refers to them in the plural, **ecclesiae**, churches in Corinth or Rome or Galatia. But the Epistle to the Ephesians gives articulate expression to the Pauline doctrine of the one universal church, the one fellowship of the Spirit, of which the local churches are manifestations. Nothing is said of ecclesiastical organization or institution. What is of constitutive importance is "the unity of the Spirit in the bond of peace," with "one Lord, one faith, one baptism, one God and Father" (Ephesians 4:3-6). This is Paul's conception of ecumenicity.

Paul's most characteristic name for the church is "the body of Christ," a figure developed not only in Ephesians but also in Romans, 1 Corinthians, and Colossians. Underlying it is the Hebrew concept of corporate personality, as when Adam includes all mankind, as well as the imagery of the Eucharist, in which Christians partake of the one loaf, the body of Christ. "Because there is one loaf," says Paul, "we, many as we are, are one body" (1 Corinthians 10:17). Paul's theology of the church as the body of Christ has both a vertical and a horizontal dimension. Applying the basic affirmation "Jesus is Lord" to the figure of the body, Paul describes Christ as the head from whom the body derives its life and growth. God "has put all things under his feet and has made him the head over all things for the church, which is his body" (Ephesians 1:22-23). "We are to grow up in every way into him who is the head, into Christ, from whom the whole body . . . makes bodily growth and upbuilds itself in love" (Ephesians 4:15-16). On the other hand, those who are members of Christ's body are also members one of another, "joined and knit together by every joint," working in harmony and interdependence for the good of the whole.

Paul thus presents a magnificent view of the church as a living organism, the body of the risen and exalted Christ, carrying out his redemptive purpose in the world. Above all, it makes Paul's ecclesiology an integral part of his Christology. As Bonhoeffer expressed it, the church is nothing less than "Christ existing in community." So close is the union of Christ with those who are "in Christ" and their unity in him that they are not merely his disciples and followers. They are parts of his living body, ingredients of the life of Christ on earth.

Whether Paul speaks of life in faith, life in the Spirit, or life in the church, the center is always Christ. His radical Christ-centered approach prevents the Christian experience of God from becoming vague man-centered religiosity. The Spirit is not satisfied with making men religious. He leads them to a personal commitment to Christ in the fellowship of his people. The gospel which introduces us to Christ is neither a code of laws nor a set of morals but the communication of Christ's resurrection power. And the Christ of the Christian faith is not a historical figure whose teachings we are asked to accept and whose example we are asked to follow. He is the risen Lord, the living and life-changing Christ present in the community of believers, working in and through them to reap the fruits of his victory over sin and death. Such is the nature of salvation in present experience, the process of being saved.

CHAPTER FIVE

Salvation as Hope

Salvation is the fundamental concept of Paul's theology but salvation, even as present experience, can be understood only when it is viewed in an eschatological perspective. Paul's doctrine of man derives its dimension of depth from his eschatology. To interpret human experience in mere psychological terms is superficial. Man is flesh and spirit but these are cosmic powers. Corresponding to them are the antitheses: grace versus law, spirit versus letter, new covenant versus old covenant, freedom versus slavery. Existence is determined by who is Lord. Everyone is caught in a change of aeons, in the transition of dominion from the principalities and powers of the present age to the rule of Christ. Man in the present fallen world is flesh, but the Spirit of the risen and exalted Christ comes to him from the outside, places him under his true Lord, and gives him existence in the world to come. Man is thus saved from sin and death, from slavery to law and the bondage of corruption. But the full consummation of salvation is in the future. It awaits the cosmic fulfilment of God's redemptive purpose. Salvation thus has the double aspect of "already" and "not yet."

Futuristic and Realized Eshatology

Both exegetical and systematic theologians are generally agreed that Pauline theology is thoroughly eschatological, but debate still goes on over the question of which of the two aspects, present or future, is dominant. The earlier epistles, especially First and Second Thessalonians, are clearly futuristic, while the later epistles, especially Romans and Colossians, shift the emphasis from expectation of the speedy and dramatic return of Christ to eternal life under the lordship of Christ experienced here and now.

In the Thessalonian letters the imminent **parousia** (the return of Christ) is portrayed in the imagery of the Jewish apocalyptic. "The Lord himself will descend from heaven with a cry of command, with the archangel's call, and with the sound of the trumpet of God" (1 Thessalonians 4:16). "The Lord Jesus is revealed from heaven with his mighty angels in flaming fire inflicting vengeance upon those who do not know God" (2 Thessalonians 1:7-8). Sharing the fervent expectancy of the first Christians that the coming of the Lord would occur during their own lifetime, Paul hopes that he would not have to fall into the sleep of death but would be among those who will be privileged to go directly "to meet the Lord in the air" (1 Thessalonians 4:17). So deeply were the Thessalonians stirred by Paul's words "concerning the coming of our Lord Jesus and our assembling to meet him" that the apostle was obliged in the second letter to warn them against being "quickly shaken in mind or excited" (2 Thessalonians 2:1-2) and to give practical instructions for living in the present world.

But the expectation of the parousia continues to condition Paul's thought even in the later epistles, as when he writes to the Corinthians: "The appointed time has grown very short; from now on, let those who have wives live as though they had none, and those who mourn as though they were not mourning, and those who rejoice as though they were not rejoicing, and those who buy as though they had no goods, and those who deal with the world as though they had no dealings with it, for the form of this world is passing away" (1 Corinthians 7:29-31). But while the apostle expects the parousia to occur in the near future ("the time has grown very short"), ("the form of this world **is passing** away") indicates that he is speaking about the coming of a new world which is already taking place. Where the Spirit creates new life, there the power of the world to come already breaks through into the old world and exposes its transitory character. Through communion with Christ the believer walks in "newness of life," a new leaf. In principle he is detached from the affairs of the old world and oriented to the new. Eschatology in this sense is not confined to "the last things." It may be described as "realized" (Dodd) or "trasmuted" (von Dobschütz) or "inaugurated" (Hunter) eschatology.

Today the futuristic interpretation is advocated most strongly by the "hope" theologians such as Moltmann and Pannenberg. Here eschatology as hope for the future is the sum and substance of all theology. The very being of God and of his kingdom is defined in terms of the future. The accent falls on the **promises** of God as symbols of the infinite possibilities lying ahead. The claim is that Paul, as well as the whole apostolic church, is willing to let go of the present in favor of the kingdom that is coming. The genesis of the gospel is in the Jewish apocalyptic with its expectation of an imminent catastrophic destruction of the present world and the inauguration of God's kingdom. Dissatisfaction with the present order and complete orientation to the future gives this kind of theology a revolutionary messianic fervor. It is the "liberation theology," giving hope to the oppressed and disadvantaged. But its failure to establish any positive link between the present and the future makes it necessary to supplement the gospel from other sources such as Marxism.

Before the rise of the "hope" theology, an interpretation of the original Christian message in terms of futuristic eschatology had already been given to Albert Schweitzer. To Schweitzer Jesus was an apocalyptist who expected the end of the world to occur during his own generation. He was the herald of a new kingdom which was to appear suddenly and miraculously and supplant the existing world-order. When he found that he was mistaken, he began voluntarily to seek his own death as the necessary birth pangs of the new age. Paul inherited from Jesus the idea of an imminent parousia. He believed that the death and resurrection of Jesus would at once usher in the new age. It was the failure of the new kingdom to arrive that led Paul to develop his concept of "being in Christ" in the present age.

Against Schweitzer, C. H. Dodd contended that neither Jesus nor Paul was mistaken. With Jesus' death and resurrection the "age to come" did arrive, and eschatology was "realized" as much as it ever would be in history. "Being in Christ" is not a Pauline afterthought. It stands for the fact that the believer already participates in the kingdom. He is crucified with Christ and risen with Christ into the new aeon. Here is the true depth of Paul's doctrine of justification. "He was raised for our justification" (Romans 4:25). Those who are "in Christ" have already appeared before the judgment throne of God and won acquittal. The coming judgment has lost its terrifying aspect, for "there is no condemnation for those who are in Christ Jesus" (Romans 8:1). For them the future has become present. The coming kingdom is no longer a distant dream but an experienced reality. Upon them "the end of the ages has come" (1 Corinthians 10:11). They have been "delivered out of the present evil age" (Galatians 1:4) and "are being changed into his likeness from one degree of glory to another" (2 Corinthians 3:18). "He has delivered us from the dominion of darkness and transferred us to the kingdom of his beloved Son" (Colossians 1:13). As a guarantee of full salvation believers already possess the Holy Spirit promised for the last days and are bringing forth the first fruits of the new resurrection life (Romans 8:23).

Both the futuristic and the "realized" aspects of Pauline eschatology must be acknowledged. The question of which line of thought is dominant is largely a question of whether Paul's thinking is rooted in Jewish or Greek concepts. The futuristic interpretation rests on the assumption that the parousia is central and is to be understood in terms of Jewish apocalyptic. This interpretation is supported by the theology of **Heilsgeschichte**, redemption history, represented by Oscar Cullmann. Here the biblical concept of redemption, as contrasted with the Greek, is tied to historical events occurring in the linear time and culminating in the final event, the parousia. Dodd, on the other hand, admits that the early Paul of the Thessalonian letters was under the influence of Jewish apocalyptic, but that the mature Paul thought of the coming kingdom in Platonic fashion, in non-temporal terms, of eternity invading time. Bultmann accepts the apocalyptic as valid but demythologizes it and interprets it, following Kierkegaard and Heidegger, as personal existential confrontation with God, eternity entering time in the present experience of the believer. Ebeling, likewise, retains the eschatological element in Paul as the "now of eternity," the dimension of eternity in present faith.

Contemporary biblical research on the whole does not posit a sharp either-or between the futuristic and the "realized" interpretations. As Kümmel points out, both aspects of eschatology are equally and permanently present in Paul's thinking, now the one and now the other being in the foreground. The evidence presented by the exponents of "realized" eschatology is incontrovertible, but their hypothesis of the Hellenization of Paul's thought remains unproven and they fail to appreciate the Old Testament conditioning of the Pauline concepts of man, of corporate solidarity (that is, of being in the first Adam and in the last Adam), of time, and of history.

On the other hand, the futurists have failed to establish the relevance of the gospel to the present age but they have brought out the focal importance of the resurrection of Christ and of the parousia as objective events which hold the key to the meaning of union with Christ.

Paul himself is unaware of any tension in the two points of view. Christ has not only risen but already reigns, although his lordship is visible only to the eyes of faith. Believers have risen with him into the new kingdom and live under his lordship but they also anticipate the parousia when the invisible becomes visible and salvation is fully consummated.

Death

Salvation as future hope involves the end of individual life at death as well as the end of all things. What is Paul's teaching on the meaning of death?

The starting-point is that death is a curse which entered the world as a result of man's disobedience to God. Paul derived this view from Genesis and develops it in Romans 5, where the key word is "the wages of sin is death." The curse "reigns" over the whole human race and encompasses the whole existence of each individual. Death is God's judgment upon man as sinner and from this judgment there is no appeal. Death is nothing natural like birth but an unnatural disruption of life in God for which man was created. Death is a demonic power which must be overthrown, the last enemy to be conquered.

The good news of the Christian message is that through the resurrection of Christ the enemy has indeed been conquered and the curse has been lifted. Were this not so, Christian faith would be a delusion and the fate of Christians at death would be annihilation (1 Corinthians 15:17-18). But Christ has in fact won the decisive victory, and death is a defeated enemy. "O death, where is thy victory? O death, where is thy sting?" (1 Corinthians 15:55). Sharing the resurrection victory, the believer can say, "for me to live is Christ and to die is gain" (Philippians 1:21). "If we live, we live to the Lord, and if we die, we die to the Lord; so then whether we live or whether we die, we are the Lord's" (Romans 14:8).

The all-important consideration, then, in facing death is the basic Pauline principle of "being in Christ." Unlike Plato, Paul knows nothing about an immortality of the soul, the inherent capacity of man as man to withstand the destructive power of death, to leap over the grave into a new existence. The question is not: as a human being am I capable of surviving death? It is this: am I a new man in Christ and therefore assured that nothing, not even death, can separate me from him? "For I am sure that neither death nor life . . . nor anything else in all creation will be able to separate us from the love of God in Christ Jesus our Lord" (Romans 8:38-39). The Spirit binds believers to their Lord and to one another with ties of faith and love which death cannot break. Christ alone "has immortality" (1 Timothy 6:16), while ours is a "mortal nature" which must "put on immortality" as his gift (1 Corinthians 15:54). To be in Christ, whether in life or in death, gives the concept of human immortality its only positive content before the final resurrection.

What happens, then, at death to one who is in Christ? Paul's answer is that he is still in Christ but out of the body. He speaks of death as a departure of the soul or spirit from the body. "My desire is to depart and to be with Christ . . . But to remain in the flesh is more necessary on your account" (Philippians 1:23-24). "We would rather be away from the body and at home with the Lord" (2 Corinthians 5:8). Paul thus affirms the possibility that the soul may continue to exist apart from the body, but he does not share

Plato's view of death as a release of the soul from the fetters of the body to live on its own and in its own proper sphere. Existence after death has a positive meaning only if it is "to be with Christ."

Furthermore, Paul cannot conceive of a protracted existence of the departed soul in a disembodied state. "For we know that if the earthly tent we live in is destroyed, we have a building from God, a house not made with hands, eternal in the heavens ... We long to put on our heavenly dwelling, so that by putting it on we may not be found naked" (2 Corinthians 5:1-3). The soul moves at death into a new dwelling to continue its life there. The new dwelling resembles the glorified resurrection body of Christ, of which Paul had a vision on the Damascus road. Christ "will change our lowly body to be like his glorious body" (Philippians 3:21). We shall not only be with Christ but also become more and more like Christ. "Just as we have borne the image of the man of dust, we shall also bear the image of the man of heaven" (1 Corinthians 15:49). When Paul speaks of this transformation in 1 Corinthians 15, it is in the context of the resurrection of the dead at the parousia. But in 2 Corinthians 5 the destruction of the "earthly tent" and the "putting on the heavenly dwelling" refer clearly to the death of the individual believer.

The transformation thus occurs at death but it continues after death. There is in fact a continuity between eternal life as a present possession and its future consummation, for the work of the Holy Spirit who "shapes us into the likeness of God's Son" (Romans 8:29) is not disrupted by death. As the resurrection power of Christ already at work, the Spirit gives fuller life and greater Christlikeness to those who die in Christ. "If the Spirit of him who raised Jesus from the dead dwells in you, he who raised Christ Jesus from the dead will give life to your mortal bodies also through his Spirit which dwells in you" (Romans 8:11). We are thus "being changed into his likeness from one degree of glory to another" (2 Corinthians 3:18) until the work of the Spirit reaches its perfection in the resurrection of the dead.

The metaphor which Paul uses most often in speaking of death is sleep. The idea of soul-sleeping, however, is foreign to him and to the entire New Testament. The apostle shares instead the conception prevalent in antiquity that in sleep the soul leaves the body and has conscious experiences outside it. The same pattern of thought appears in Paul's references to his ecstatic visions: "whether in the body or out of the body I do not know" (2 Corinthians 12:2-3). Falling asleep in Christ or departing from the body to be with Christ would thus be a prolongation of this ecstatic condition. The blessed dead are with Christ and enjoy his presence. But this is not a normal condition. Even ecstatic sleep is not an adequate substitute for full-bodied participation in the heavenly life. Paul shudders at the idea of disembodied existence, of being found naked, and expects a new spiritual body at death. Distinguishing between this body and the final resurrection body, Schleiermacher projected the concept of a **Zwischenleib**, a temporary body occupied before the resurrection. And Martensen wondered whether a new body might not already be in the making within the present body, nourished by the Eucharist and ready for occupation at death. Paul does not engage in such speculation, although he does not reject the idea of an intermediate state, which he inherited from the kerygma of the church and which is clearly present in the accounts of Moses and Elijah appearing on the mount of transfiguration, of Lazarus in "Abraham's bosom," and of the dying thief who was to be with Jesus in paradise.

Paul Althaus, in his influential **Die letzten Dinge**, represents many modern theologians for whom there is no problem here, for they reject the intermediate state altogether. The whole man, body and soul, dies, and the whole man, body and soul, is resurrected on the last day. There is no period of waiting, for waiting implies time, and beyond death time no longer has any significance. We may say that departed believers are at home with the Lord in the sense that their striving and waiting are over and they have reached their goal. But the dead are in a category of timelessness in which the end of time for an individual is indistinguishable from the end of history. It is questionable, however, whether such an interpretation does justice to what Paul expected at death. If we cannot define the realization of his hope to depart and be with his Lord in a more constructive way than to say that he is in a timeless instant and without body or soul, then it is best to say nothing at all.

The Final Consummation

Paul's conviction that at death he would move from an ''earthly tent'' into a ''heavenly dwelling'' and enter into a closer communion with his Lord does not in any way weaken his expectation of the parousia, the return of Christ, when God's purpose for his whole creation will be fully realized. Although this may not take place during his own life-time, as the Apostle hopes, he continues to stress: ''The Lord is at hand'' (Philippians 4:5),''the appointed time has grown very short'' (1 Corinthians 7:29), the consummation of salvation is rapidly approaching, it is ''nearer to us now than when we first believed'' (Romans 13:11). In Romans 8 he gives magnificent expression to the Christian hope. He describes Christians as being sustained in the midst of the sufferings of the present time by the expectancy of the glory to be revealed. He goes on to portray the whole world as standing on tiptoe waiting with eager longing for the unfolding of the divine purpose. Using another image he compares all creation to a woman writhing and groaning in labor pains, anxious for the appearance of the new life of the future.

Paul's portrayal of the final climactic act of the drama of history may be sketched in brief outline. Christ will descend from heaven with great power and glory, surrounded by his holy angels. The dead in Christ will rise from their graves. The believers who are still living will be transformed and will join the whole host of the Lord's own to meet him. The forces of Christ and of the Antichrist will engage in decisive combat. "The Lord Jesus will slay the man of lawlessness with the breath of his mouth and destroy him" (2 Thessalonians 2:8). All principalities and powers will bow before Christ. The last enemy to be destroyed is death. All the dead will be resurrected and will appear before the judgment throne of Christ. Christ will then deliver the kingdom to God the Father and God will be everything to everyone.

Beside the triumph of Christ, there are two outstanding features in this portrayal — resurrection and judgment. The Corinthian Christians to whom Paul wrote at length about the resurrection of the dead were familiar with the Greek idea of immortality, but the Jewish idea of resurrection was strange to them. He therefore expected them to ask, "How are the dead raised? With what kind of body do they come?" (1 Corinthians 15:35). Paul rejects sharply the notion that the body which was buried in the grave will rise, that resurrection will be a revivification of physical relics. "Flesh and blood cannot inherit the kingdom of God" (1 Corinthians 15:50). Yet Paul's hope is not in an immortality of the soul but in the God "who gives life to the dead and calls into existence the things that do not exist" (Romans 4:17). There is no genuine human existence without a body, but the God who gave me a body suited to earthly existence can also give me a body suited to heavenly existence. There are various kinds of bodies, earthly and heavenly, perishable and imperishable. Yet there is a continuity between the earthly body and the heavenly body just as there is between the seed sown in the ground and the new sprout which rises from it. The prototype of the new body is the resurrection body of Christ. God will change our lowly body to be like his glorious body. The perishable will thus put on the imperishable, and mortality will put on immortality.

The resurrection of the dead is followed by the last judgment. "God," says Paul, "shall judge the secrets of men by Jesus Christ" (Romans 2:16). "We shall all stand before the judgment seat of God." (Romans 14:10). Since believers have already been acquitted by God's grace, they face the judgment seat with the assurance: "There is no **katakrima** (judgment of condemnation) for those who are in Christ Jesus" (Romans 8:1). But the believer is not allowed, any more than the unbeliever, to enter his final destiny with a false estimate of himself, as Paul points out in a remarkable passage: "For no other foundation can anyone lay than that which is laid, which is Jesus Christ. Now if anyone builds on the foundation with gold, silver, precious stones, wood, hay, stubble — each man's work will become manifest; for the Day will disclose it, because it will be revealed with fire, and the fire will test what sort of work each has done. If the work which any man has built on the foundation survives, he will receive a reward. If any man's work is burned up, he will suffer loss, though he himself will be saved, but only as through fire" (1 Corinthians 3:11-15). This is a description of the judgment of believers, for each man has built on Christ as the foundation. The believer who has built of gold, silver, or precious stones has shown the true mind of Christ and performed works of love. But when a Christian has sought his own glory, had vain pretensions, and lacked the mind of Christ, he has built of wood, hay, and stubble, which the fire of judgment will destroy. While his guilt is thus made manifest, the forgiveness of sins in Christ still holds and he is saved. But he will be chastened and humble as he enters heaven.

What about the fate of unbelievers? There are statements which seem to indicate that Paul believed in **apokatastasis**, the ultimate redemption of all men. "God has consigned all men to disobedience that he may have mercy upon all" (Romans 11:32). God's purpose is "to reconcile to himself all things, whether on earth or in heaven" (Colossians 1:20). The ultimate goal is "that God may be everything to everyone" (1 Corinthians 15:28). These statements, however, cannot be detached from the rest of Paul's teaching and made to support universalism. The contexts show that Paul is speaking of the universal nature and offer of the salvation accomplished in Christ, which many reject and are lost. In Romans 11, where he speaks of "mercy for all" he is thinking of races, not individuals. He is especially concerned with his own "kinsmen according to the flesh." It is his fervent desire and prayer that all Israel will be saved, and he is willing even to sacrifice his own personal salvation for this end. But when he reflects on the rejection of Christ by the Jews, he declares that "God's wrath has come upon them finally and completely" (1 Thessalonians 2:16). "Those who do not obey the gospel of our Lord Jesus," says Paul, "shall suffer the punishment of eternal destruction and exclusion from the presence of the Lord" (2 Thessalonians 1:9). Far from teaching that all men, whether they have faith in Christ or not, will be saved, Paul draws a distinction between those who "are being saved" and those who "are perishing" (2 Corinthians 2:15).

In the depths of his heart Paul appears to have entertained the hope that love, the most abiding of all realities, would have the last word in the case of everyone of God's creatures and that in the end the God of love would be everything to everyone. But he was also in grave earnest about the possibility of eternal perdition. He does not presume to know the answers to all ultimate questions. "Who has known the mind of the Lord? How unsearchable are his judgments and how inscrutable his ways!" (Romans 11:33-34). On the last things in particular "our knowledge is imperfect and our prophecy is imperfect" and "we see in a mirror dimly" (1 Corinthians 13:9, 12). But this we know: "What no eye has seen, nor ear heard, nor the heart of man conceived, what God has prepared for those who love him, God has revealed to us through the Spirit" (1 Corinthians 2:9-10).

CHAPTER SIX

Paul Today

The task that remains is to summarize our study of Paul's theology and to make a specific application of it to the present day. Our point of view has been to regard Paul as the foremost theologian of the early church, the supreme interpreter of Jesus and his gospel to the world of his day. He was not, as liberals at the beginning of the present century thought, the second founder of Christianity who introduced dogma and mysticism to transform Jesus' simple message of the fatherhood of God and the brotherhood of man into a cosmic drama of redemption. Paul's theology is rooted in Jesus' proclamation of the coming of God's kingdom, now fulfilled in his death and resurrection. In the succeeding centuries this theology became, as James Denney put it, "incomparably the greatest source of spiritual revivals in the Christian Church." [24] But is it still vital and relevant in our day?

The Human Predicament

Let us consider first whether we can agree with Paul's analysis of the human predicament. For Paul, as for all of Scripture, the starting point for this analysis is God, not man. Human existence is to be defined in terms of its relationship to God. Man is because God is. "In him we live and move and have our being" (Acts 17:28). Man was created for fellowship with God and only in God does he realize his destiny. But the fellowship has been broken by sin, and the human condition is one of alienation from him who gives meaning and purpose to life. "All have sinned and fall short of the glory of God" (Romans 3:23). "God has consigned all men to disobedience"

(Romans 11:32). "Death spread to all men because all men sinned" (Romans 5:12). In presenting the gospel we must therefore begin with the fact of a fallen world and the deadly power of sin which no man can overcome.

Is this a true description of the human predicament, one which we can still accept nineteen centuries after Paul? Is not the fall into sin an ancient myth which has no place in modern scientific analysis of human nature? Ignorant of the laws of heredity, did not Paul falsely assume that the guilt of Adam could be inherited? How can we speak of "original sin" when psychological studies have failed to find any trace of "sin" in the original equipment with which a human being starts life? And how can an enlightened ethics hold us responsible for an act committed by one man in the dawn of history?

In confronting these questions we must admit that they represent what Paul would call the "scandal" of the Christian message and that Brunner is right in saying that the doctrine of original sin is a primary form of that scandal for modern man. The objections, however, do not touch the depth of the scandal, Paul's diagnosis of original sin as a perennial human predicament, his view of human existence as such as being geared wrong to ultimate reality. His analysis goes deeper than historical account, empirical description, or ethical evaluation. Original sin is a purely religious concept which discloses that man, with all his wisdom, morality, and progress, is a rebel against God, and that the rebellion goes on from generation to generation. This insight is lost in the attempt to take Genesis 3 as literal history. In the words of Archibald Hunter, "we know that Adam is Hebrew for a human being or mankind collectively, and that Genesis 3 is to be regarded as a 'true myth,' that, though Eden is on no map and Adam's fall fits no historical calendar, that chapter witnesses to a dimension of human experience as real now as at the beginning of man's story — in plain terms, we are fallen creatures and the tale of Adam and Eve is the story of you and me."[25] There is nothing paradoxical about "true myth"; for myth, used here as in Plato, is not fiction but a vehicle of profound truth.

In keeping with the Hebrew concept of corporate personality, Paul constantly uses Adam to denote humanity as a whole, just as he refers to the new humanity as being in the last Adam, Christ. He affirms that "sin came into the world through one man" but he does not teach that sin is biologically inherited. All men, beginning with the first man, are sinners but every man is responsible for his own sin. Paul refers to the ultimate origin of the rebellion against God in a transcendent demonic realm, "the spiritual hosts of wickedness in the heavenly places." But instead of prying into the "mystery of iniquity," whether in the fall of Satan or of Adam, he simply affirms the reality of a radical kink of evil in human nature which only God can straighten out. It is worth noting that Kant, the profoundest modern analyst of man's moral spoke likewise of "Radical evil."

When I began my study of theology more than a half century ago, the idea of original sin was regarded as an anachronism. A mood of evolutionary optimism prevailed. The only truth which original sin was held to represent was that human nature still retains some relics of our brutish ancestry but these will disappear as the human race progresses upward and onward. Sin is ignorance which better education will cure. It is psychological maladjustment which better psychology will eliminate. It is perpetuated by corrupt social institutions which better social engineering will remake. We therefore no longer ask, "Wretched man that I am, who will deliver me?" but "Progressive creature that I am, who will help me to realize myself?"

Today's mood is far more sober. The utopian dreams of yesterday have turned into nightmares. The horrible destruction of war, the decay of morals, the soaring crime rate, the corruption on the highest levels of government — these are symptoms of a disease residing in the very bone and marrow of human existence, incurable by methods born of false optimism. Theologians now recognize that Niebuhr's restoration of the Pauline diagnosis of human nature is sounder than the liberalism which he attacked and that Tillich's description of the demonization of life is more than fantasy. To a disillusioned and bewildered generation such as ours, haunted by the chaotic meaninglessness of life, the gospel of Paul is highly relevant. It is not a call for men to develop their own spiritual potentialities but honestly to admit failure and to accept rescue coming from beyond themselves, the grace of God offered to men who are estranged from him.

The Divine Rescue

If Paul's diagnosis of the human predicament is still relevant, can the same be said about the cure which he offers? We cannot save ourselves, says Paul, but God has done for us what we cannot do. We are "justified by his grace as a gift, through the redemption which is in Christ Jesus" (Romans 3:24). "God shows his love for us in that while we were yet sinners, Christ died for us" (Romans 5:8). God takes the initiative. He seeks man whether man seeks him or not. His saving love encompasses man in the midst of his estrangement. He justifies the ungodly. He acquits the guilty. He receives the sinner into fellowship with himself, for he has it in his heart to love sinners as they are.

What happens when this gospel is preached to the men and women of our generation?

Unfortunately, in many cases, nothing. Missing are the unspeakable joy and wonder and the radical personality-change which Paul experienced when he was overwhelmed by "amazing grace" and which his converts experienced as they passed over from heathenism into Christianity. Something of this is still evident when the gospel makes its impact upon persons who have never heard of Christ or have lived godless lives. But the "power of God unto salvation" has little reality to those who have been brought up in conventional Christian homes and are familiar with Christian teaching from early childhood. As Stanley Jones used to say, they have been so inoculated with small doses that the real thing does not take. They feel no sense of guilt or need of conversion. As a physician in one of our churches told his pastor, "I cannot participate in the confession of sins, because I have never been unfaithful to my wife." And where sin is acknowledged, it is easily covered with what Bonhoeffer called "cheap grace" which perverts justification of the sinner into justification of sin. Few would go so far as to say openly with Heinrich Heine, "I like to sin, God likes to forgive sin, a convenient arrangement." But the underlying attitude that the "man upstairs" is a kindly grandfather who looks through his fingers at our peccadilloes is more prevalent than we like to think.

Paul was keenly aware of the possibility of such antinomian perversion of the doctrine of grace. His answer to the question, "Are we to continue in sin that grace may abound?", was a horrified "God forbid!" and he went on to portray the newness of life in grace in terms comparable only to the resurrection of Christ from the dead (Romans 6:1-3).

Paul's analogy of dying and rising with Christ is certainly a powerful figure for expressing the entrance into the new life. But to modern men it appears to be more a flight of poetic imagination than a description of actual experience. Paul's other thought patterns seem just as remote. The grand words "redemption" and "justification" which Paul used and which theologians have continued to use through the centuries no longer "ring a bell." When Paul spoke of redemption, the word brought home the message of liberation to his hearers who were familiar with the purchase of freedom for a slave. To us it only suggests a redemption center where green stamps can be exchanged for merchandise. And justification does not lift the curtain on an impressive courtroom scene where the judge pronounces acquittal for one who has been found guilty. For us it is vindication of one's conduct or finding excuses for it. Every term in the Pauline message of the justification of the sinner by grace through faith has undergone this kind of linguistic erosion. For Paul faith meant the restoration of a confident personal relationship to God and the ensuing life of commitment and obedience. For the popular mind today it means either believing what cannot be verified or optimistic self-confidence or sentimental religiosity, "when I hear a newborn baby cry, I believe." Sin has come to mean this or that act of moral failure, not the total life-attitude of rebellion against God. Grace is now a winsome geniality in the nature of God which renders the idea of his "wrath" obsolete, not a saving holy love bestowed upon those who have deserved only his righteous wrath. Instead of the superficial "God hates sin but loves sinners" Paul teaches that the sinner himself, not sin in the abstract, has incurred divine judgment but receives divine pardon.

The Pauline word which is best suited to convey his gospel to modern men is "reconciliation." "God was in Christ reconciling the world to himself . . . We beseech you on behalf of Christ, be reconciled to God" (2 Corinthians 5:19-20). Here is a way of speaking which is never out of date and is relevant wherever human hearts throb. It is the language, not of the slave-market or the courtroom, but of human relations. Our Lord himself in his greatest parable preserved the message of reconciliation in terms of forgiving love which brings about the restoration of a father-son relationship. The Father who runs down the road to embrace his wayward son is the God whom Paul describes as justifying the ungodly and acquitting the guilty. We cannot escape the conclusion reached by Wesley and Aulen and Jeremias that the whole doctrine of redemption, justification, and reconciliation may be summed up in the word "forgiveness." What Paul tells us through various figures of speech is that unless God forgives us we remain estranged from him and are lost. And like his Lord he goes on to stress, "As God has forgiven you, you too must forgive" (Colossians 3:13). This gospel of reconciliation through forgiveness is still the answer to broken personal relations between God and man and between man and man.

Faith and Works

What about Paul's emphasis on faith, over against works, as the way of salvation? Is it something incidental, a revolt of the apostle against his Jewish background, or does it still have relevance? Let us admit that works-righteousness, dependence on the performance of duty, always has been and still is the religion of natural man. People both in the churches and outside the churches believe that if a man does the best he can to fulfill his obligations, God will overlook his mistakes and regard him with favor. Kierkegaard uses the myth of the heaven-storming Prometheus to show that man will do anything to enter heaven by his own effort. For Calvin the strongest proof of God's omnipotence is that he can bring a sinner to his knees to accept salvation as a free gift.

The American tradition in particular has been a stubborn determination to achieve on one's own. A premium has been placed on individual resourcefulness and hard work, taking advantage of the opportunity to get ahead and enjoying the satisfaction of knowing, "I did it my way." I still remember vividly the advice given by the school superintendent at my graduation from high school. "Blaze your own trail," he said, "clear your own plantation," and he used the illustration of Ty Cobb ferociously stealing bases without waiting for someone else to advance him. Self-reliance, we were told, is the key to success.

American religious thought has been cast in this mold from the beginning. Its original determinants were the legalism and the work-ethic of the Puritans and the anti-supernaturalistic rationalism of the eighteenth century Enlightenment, the philosophy of the founding fathers of our democracy. The resultant attitude is that of the people to whom the parable of the Pharisee and the publican was first told: "they trusted in themselves that they were righteous" (Luke 18·9).

"Both Jesus and Paul agree," says Jeremias, "that no man is so far from God as the self-righteous person."[26] The gospel of sin and grace begins to make sense only when man has become his own biggest problem, when he realizes that with all his achievements his orientation to life is wrong, that he needs God but his whole life is in contradiction to God. Today we are recovering the awareness of the need for a radical change in basic life-attitude. Mass evangelism has returned to popularity, for it seeks to meet this need in its own simplistic emotional fashion. But it is also explored in depth by both theologians and psychologists. Niebuhr's profound analysis of the nature of man as sinner finds its psychological counterpart in Menninger's insistence that sin must be taken seriously. Kunkel has pointed out that egocentrism casts a poisonous cloak on man's search for spiritual maturity and that the egocentric axis must be broken if the true self is to emerge. Karen Horney saw in preoccupation with self the distinctive trait of the neurotic personality of our time. Paul's gospel thus speaks to contemporary man in his actual condition. He needs to find a center of life beyond himself. He needs to discover with the apostle the new life which leads him to say, "The life I now live is not my own life but the life which Christ lives in me" (Galatians 2:20).

If Paul speaks meaningfully to men of today about the need of a new life, can the same be said about the content of the new life? For Paul its basic content is "to be in Christ." "For me to live is Christ." Christ is the source and the goal, the norm and the **enabler, the very "raison d'etre" of life.** Paul's life-purpose is "to know him and the power of his resurrection" and "to become like him" through an ever deepening fellowship with him. Is it possible for us to have such total involvement with one who lived two thousand years ago in a far-away land? There are those who believe that authentic Christianity is a harking back to the first century in the attempt to follow Jesus as his first disciples did in Galilee. But that is not what Paul meant by being in Christ. He did not know the historical Jesus and he did not want to know him "after the flesh." His Lord was the triumphant and living "last Adam" who had become the life-giving Spirit. It is the Holy Spirit who makes Christ the contemporary of men of every age.

The Work of the Holy Spirit

Phillips Brooks was once asked whether communion with Christ is necessary if one is to be a Christian. His reply was, "Communion with Christ **is** Christianity." This is precisely what Paul teaches. But since communion with Christ is the work of the Holy

Spirit, the discovery of the reality of the Holy Spirit is as vital a necessity in the twentieth century as in the first. Paul's writings are radiant with the Spirit, for the Christian era is a "dispensation of the Spirit," Christian life is "walking by the Spirit," Christian virtues are the "fruits of the Spirit," Christian skills are the "gifts of the Spirit," and the Christian hope is realized through "the Spirit of him who raised Christ Jesus from the dead." If this is not a description of today's Christianity, it is because the essential factor, the Holy Spirit, is missing. An awakened awareness of this fact accounts for the spread of the "charismatic movement" from the Pentecostal sects into the established churches. This interest in the work of the Spirit is a wholesome reaction against the lifeless formalism and traditionalism into which the churches tend to fall. But if it is to produce lasting results and not evaporate into transitory emotionalism, as has been the case with many holiness movements in the past, it cannot afford to disregard the theological guidelines which Paul offers. Such great chapters as Romans 8, 1 Corinthians 12-14, 2 Corinthians 3, and Galatians 5 must be studied anew and the apostolic insights must be applied constructively to the present situation.

Three of these insights are especially important. First, the work of Christ is the foundation for the work of the Spirit. The doctrine of the Holy Spirit is a Christological doctrine. The indwelling Spirit is the indwelling Christ. Paul's words must be kept in mind: "The Lord is the Spirit" (2 Corinthians 3:17) and "Anyone who does not have the Spirit of Christ does not belong to him" (Romans 8:9). The Spirit teaches and imparts the mind of Christ and makes Christ a personally experienced reality. The intimate relation between the Spirit and Christ makes the doctrine of the Spirit both existential and objective. It calls for an actual confrontation with the living Christ but it is also an effective safeguard against identifying the Spirit with any form of human spirituality and subjective emotionalism.

The second insight is that the work of the Spirit is inseparably connected with the fellowship of the Spirit, the community of believers, the church. The **charis** of the Lord Jesus Christ and the **agape** of God are experienced in the **koinonia** of the Holy Spirit (2 Corinthians 13:13). Life in Christ is a life shared with all others who are in Christ. Individual communion with Christ is not something to be enjoyed for one's personal satisfaction; it is meaningful only if it enriches the whole fellowship. Thus the criterion for judging the "gifts of the Spirit" is this: are these experiences divisive or do they edify the church? When Paul hears of divisions and "parties" in the church, he is horrified. "Is Christ divided?" he asks. There is but one Christ, and Christ has but one body, the church. For Paul all genuine Christian experience is churchly experience. But he also calls us to a recovery of the unity of the church, a healing of the broken body of Christ.

The third insight is the primacy of **agape** as the highest of the gifts of the Spirit and the impelling motive of the Christian life. The nature of the Pauline agape is masterfully portrayed in Nygren's classic, **Eros and Agape**. It is spontaneous and unconditioned, welling up from the depths of God's own being, not seeking but creating worth in its object. It is God's way to man, not man's way to God. It is God himself at work in and through men. Were we to follow Kierkegaard's suggestion that the Christian life is a "reduplication" of the Christ-life in the life of the believer, we could substitute our own name for the word **agape** in 1 Corinthians 13. Using the New English Bible we would then have this description of a Christian man: "John is patient, John is kind and envies no one. John is never boastful, nor conceited, nor rude, never selfish, not quick to take offense. John keeps no score of wrongs; he does not gloat over other men's sins, but delights in the truth. There is nothing John cannot face, there is no limit to his faith, his hope, and his endurance." Obviously we have here a transcendent ideal rather than an empirical fact, although a saint like John XXIII came close to fitting the description. Paul himself would say, "Not that I have already obtained this or am already perfect, but I press on to make it my own, because Christ Jesus has made me his own" (Philippians 3:12).

For Paul agape is the governing principle not only in individual life but in all human relations. "Agape does no wrong to a neighbor; therefore agape is the fulfilling of the law" (Romans 13:10). Here is a law of life which time cannot render obsolete, which is as valid today as it was to Paul's readers in Rome or Corinth. Admittedly it offers no easy solution to the problems confronting us in the complex modern world. As Reinhold Niebuhr puts it, "Love is always relevant but never a simple possibility." We may recall, for example, the jeering words of Clemenceau when Wilson tried to apply this approach at Versailles, "Wilson talks like Jesus Christ." When agape was laughed out of court, seeds of hatred were sown which soon blossomed into another world war. The truth remains: other approaches end in failure, but "love never faileth." "Make agape your aim," counsels Paul. Let the tactics required by each situation vary, but never lose sight of the basic strategy. It is the strategy of agape by which God won back his lost creation and to which belongs the "love never faileth." "Make agape your aim," counsels Paul. Let the tactics required by each situation vary, but never lose sight of the basic strategy. It is the strategy of agape by which God won back his lost creation and to which belongs the future.

The Last Things

Finally, is Paul's eschatology relevant to the present day? We have seen that the apostle's teaching on "the last things" has a double aspect, the realized and the expected, the "already" and the "not yet." Through the resurrection of Christ a "breakthrough" of God's eternal kingdom into the present world has already occurred, the power of a new creation is already at work, and Christ's people have already risen with him into the new age. Upon Christ's resurrection rests everything essential in the church's message: the divinity of Christ, the forgiveness of sins, the power for a changed life, and the assurance of victory over death. This Pauline emphasis, strongly stated in such chapters as Romans 6 and 1 Corinthians 15, needs to be recaptured if the church is to be "the community of the resurrection," transmitting "the power of God unto salvation" into a world of sin and sadness and despair. The note of Christ's triumph should sound in every sermon, and every Sunday should be an Easter festival.

But Paul's eschatology is also strongly futuristic. He looks for the coming of Christ in glory, the resurrection of the dead, and the last judgment. He anticipates the complete fulfilment of God's redemptive purpose. What is the response to this kind of talk in the minds of people today? We do not have much of it in the established churches, and people do not faint in the pews as when Jonathan Edwards preached about the day of reckoning. We think of the future in terms of a better world made possible by scientific progress and social engineering. Respectable churchmen are content to relegate the second coming of Christ to the adventists and the fundamentalists.

Yet biblical scholarship today has established beyond question the fact that the original Christian message is eschatological through and through. The moralized and socialized gospel of liberal theology is not the gospel of Jesus or of Paul. As Karl Barth observed, a theology which is not eschatological has nothing to do with Christ. Thus one of the most powerful of contemporary theological trends, the theology of hope, is completely oriented to the future, convinced, as Moltmann insists, that eschatology is not just another branch of theology but the essence of all theology. There is only a tenuous connection, however, between Pauline eschatology and the secularistic utopianism and political radicalism advocated by the contemporary theologians of hope.

Paul's view of the future focuses on the parousia, the day of Christ, when the consequences of his redemptive work will be fully revealed. He shared with other Christians of his generation the ardent hope that the day of Christ would arrive during their own life-time. But as it became apparent that he would not live to see the great day, his attention shifted from the time-element to the timeless truth represented by the parousia. What is all-important is that the future belongs to Christ and that nothing in heaven or on earth can prevent his ultimate triumph.

Paul does not envision a gradual development of the kingdom of God in history but a gigantic clash between Christ and the powers opposed to him. The victory of Christ is sure, for by his resurrection he has already triumphed over all principalities and powers, and the parousia will make this triumph manifest. The same risen Christ who is the only hope of the individual Christian at death is also the hope of the entire world as it comes to its end. Just as the believer in dying does not fall into nothingness but into the arms of God, so when history has run its course, it encounters not nothingness but God in Christ. "When all things are subjected to him, then the Son himself will also be subjected to him who put all things under him, that God may be everything to everyone" (1 Corinthians 15:28).

This hope is not a vague surmise but a "solid weight of glory" which supports Christians in their present struggles. It does not lead to morbid brooding or idle dreaming but energizes us for responsibility and service. It is significant that Paul concludes his magnificent presentation of eschatology in 1 Corinthians 15 with the words: "Therefore, my beloved brethren, be steadfast, immovable, always abounding in the work of the Lord, knowing that in the Lord your labor is not in vain." And in the following verse, with the echoes of the last trumpet still reverberating, he proceeds to give practical instruction concerning contributions for the relief of the poor.

The Christian hope is faith with vision, faith with courage, faith with strength to carry on even when the situation appears hopeless. It provides the perspective of eternity in which grace, redemption, and salvation — all Christian doctrines — are to be viewed. And it gives to men in all ages the incentive for confident, consecrated, and victorious living. For "in the Lord" we have the assurance: "all things are yours, whether . . . life or death or the present or the future, all are yours; and you are Christ's; and Christ is God's" (1 Corinthians 3:21-23).

FOOTNOTES

1. Archibald M. Hunter, **The Gospel According to St Paul** (Philadelphia: Westminster Press, 1967), 11.
2. **Ibid.**, 12-13.
3. Rudolf Bultmann, **Theology of the New Testament**, Vol. I (New York: Charles Scribner's Sons, 1951), 188.
4. **The Expository Times**, October, 1964, 27-30.
5. W. G. Kümmel, **Heilsgeschehen und Geschichte** (Marburg: N. G. Elwert, 1965), 456.
6. Teilhard de Chardin, **Hymn of the Universe** (New York: Harper and Row, 1965), 36.
7. James Moffatt, **Grace in the New Testament** (New York: Ray Long and Richard R. Smith, Inc., 1932), 131.
8. **Op. cit.**, 13.
9. James Denney, **The Epistles** to the Thessalonians, The Expositor's Bible, 15.
10. **Op. cit.**, 5-6.
11. **Op. cit.**, 15.
12. **Op. cit.**, 271.
13. **Op. cit.**, 264.
14. Ficker II, 121, 10.
15. Luther's Works (Lenker edition) X, section 37.
16. Quoted by Hunter, **op. cit.**, 21.
17. Joachim Jeremias, **The Central Message of the New Testament** (New York: Charles Scribner's Sons, 1965), 57.
18. Ethelbert Stauffer, **New Testament Theology** (New York: Macmillan, 1955), 181-184, 305.
19. Adolf Deissmann, **Paul** (New York: George H. Doran, 1926), 28.
20. Rudolf Bultmann, **op. cit.**, 328.
21. **Op. cit.**, 34.
22. **Ibid.**, 36.

23. Herman Gunkel, **Die Wirkung des Heiligen Geistes**, Göttingen, 1909.
24. James Denney, **The Christian Doctrine of Reconciliation** (New York: George H. Doran, 1918), 179.
25. **Op. cit.**, 94.
26. **Expository Times**, September, 1955, 369.